Anyone who has faced a serious or chronic illness, whether physical or emotional, knows the pain and hopelessness that can engulf you. Quin and Ruthanne's book, abounding with testimonies of God's healing power, will encourage you to lay hold of the scriptural principles they share and believe God for healing and restoration. A real faith-builder!

—JANE HANSEN, PRESIDENT/CEO
AGLOW INTERNATIONAL

Quin and Ruthanne have done it again! Tastefully written, sensitive to the needs of hurting people, and so full of the life of Jesus, *Lord, I Need Your Healing Power* will be used to set captives free! This book is filled with faith, hope, and love, and it directs the reader straight to the One who can and will send help! If you have a need, this book has an answer!

—JAMES W. AND MICHAL ANN GOLL
FOUNDERS OF ENCOUNTERS NETWORK

Once again Quin Sherrer and Ruthanne Garlock have blessed us with a gem. Their ability to present deep and powerful truth in such a practical and relevant way makes this book one of their best. A great read!

—PASTOR DUTCH SHEETS
SPRINGS HARVEST FELLOWSHIP
COLORADO SPRING, COLORADO

Lord, I Need Your Healing Power is a remarkable and touching book filled with insight and inspiration that reminds us God still heals and restores broken bodies and spirits. You will find healing in these pages.

—DR. DICK EASTMAN
INTERNATIONAL PRESIDENT, EVERY HOME FOR CHRIST

Ruthanne and Quin are mature and well trained in the Bible, have traveled the world ministering to people, and have witnessed mighty answers to steadfast prayer. What makes *Lord, I Need Your Healing Power* of such interest are the personal accounts of men and women who have experienced healing. The anointed scriptures, testimonies, teachings, and prayers are all recorded in this book. It's all here! A book that will tell you how to be healed is a great treasure!

—Freda Lindsay
Cofounder and Chairman of the Board Emeritus
Christ For The Nations, Inc.
Dallas, Texas

This could well be today's handbook on healing in its most practical form, inspiring hope and quickening faith. Covering a wider spectrum than most books on the subject, Quin and Ruthanne lovingly and effectively deal with total wholeness for Christians today. I highly recommend this thoughtful, easy-to-read book that shows us that God has no cut-and-dried formulas, because He deals with each of us individually.

—Iverna Tompkins, Founder and President
Iverna Tompkins Ministries
Phoenix, Arizona

I was privileged to be the pastor who encouraged Quin Sherrer to believe in healing and to write about it more than thirty years ago—starting with Bill Lance, whose story is in chapter one. The book is packed with testimonies of those who have been touched by God's healing power. As you read it and study the Scriptures, new hope will rise in you.

—The Rev. Forrest Mobley
Immanuel Anglican Church
Destin, Florida

Lord,
I NEED YOUR
HEALING POWER

SECURING GOD'S HELP IN
SICKNESS & TRIALS

Quin Sherrer
Ruthanne Garlock

Lord,
I Need Your
Healing Power

Securing God's Help in
Sickness & Trials

Cover design by John Hamilton Design
                www.johnhamiltondesign.com

Published in association with the literary agency of Ann Spangler and Company, 1420 Pontiac Road SE, Grand Rapids, MI 49506.

Library of Congress Cataloging-in-Publication Data:

Sherrer, Quin.
  Lord, I need your healing power / Quin Sherrer and Ruthanne Garlock. -- 1st ed.
       p. cm.
   ISBN 1-59185-909-3 (trade paper)
  1. Spiritual healing. 2. Healing--Religious aspects--Christianity.
I. Garlock, Ruthanne. II. Title.
   BT732.5.S511 2006
   234'.131--dc22
                              2006019011

First Edition

06 07 08 09 10 — 9 8 7 6 5 4 3 2 1
Printed in the United States of America

*We dedicate this book to Jesus Christ our Lord, who
through His death, burial, and resurrection made
salvation and healing possible for all of us.*

*He forgives all my sins
    and heals all my diseases.
He ransoms me from death
    and surrounds me with love and tender mercies.
He fills my life with good things.
    My youth is renewed like the eagle's!*
                                    —Psalm 103:3–5, NLT

Acknowledgments

*W*E EXPRESS OUR great appreciation to:

- Ann Spangler, our friend and agent who cast the vision for this book

- Bert Ghezzi, editorial director of Strang imprints, our longtime friend who encouraged us in this project

- The team of editors and others at Charisma House who helped complete the book—especially Lillian McAnally and Ann Mulchan

- All those who shared their inspiring stories to encourage our readers

- Our prayer partners who for years have prayed faithfully for us

Quin: I wish to thank those who have taught me much about healing: Forrest Mobley, Dutch Sheets, and James and Michal Ann Goll.

Ruthanne: I wish to honor the memory of my childhood pastors, John and Lydia Stubblefield, who mentored me in faith and prayed for my healing.

Contents

Introduction

$\mathcal{S}$ICKNESS. DISEASE. ACCIDENTS. Disturbing reports from medical tests.

A roller coaster of emotions grips you when these traumas strike...fear...hopelessness...despair.

An avalanche of questions..."What to do?" "Who to turn to?" "Who can I trust?" "Who can I call for prayer?"

When health challenges hit you head-on, these emotions and questions are a natural human response. But a health crisis also gives you an opportunity to come to a deeper understanding that the same God who created your body has the power to heal it.

We hope as you read *Lord, I Need Your Healing Power* you will come to know God more intimately by one of His names: *Jehovah Rophe*, "the LORD who heals" (Exod. 15:26). The Hebrew word *rophe* means to "heal, cure, restore, or make whole." In the New Testament we read that "Jesus went throughout Galilee, teaching...preaching...and healing every disease and sickness among the people" (Matt. 4:23, NIV). And in our day He is still the Great Physician.

I (Quin) didn't know this as a young teen when I was lying sick with malaria fever for days. Medication hadn't helped. As I drifted in and out of consciousness, my worried mother soaked my body with wet towels. When she heard there were some healing evangelists at the Pentecostal church in town, she sent for them to come pray over me. From my sickbed, I awakened and looked into the faces of a black man and woman. Both were dressed in all-white clothing, and they were noisily rebuking the fever and thanking God for my complete healing. "Praise the Lord!" they kept shouting. For a moment I thought I had already died and gone to heaven. But, instinctively, I threw my feet over the side of the bed and sat up. The fever was gone, and I was perfectly well. I asked for a chocolate milk shake.

My mother's desperation had caused her to summon those "angels" with the gift of healing to come pray for me. I honestly didn't know that any believer could pray for healing—it was years later before I learned more truths about this aspect of God. But I never again had another attack of malaria.

One of my (Ruthanne's) earliest memories of being healed through prayer happened when I was about twelve years old and suffering with eczema. The doctor had prescribed some ointment that my mom helped me apply to the outbreaks every day. Also, two or three days a week after school I had to take the city bus to his office in downtown Tulsa for an injection. But the shots didn't seem to be helping.

At the Pentecostal church my family attended, our pastor often had a prayer line at the end of the Sunday evening service. On one such Sunday I was at the back of the church looking after a couple of toddlers when my mom came to get me. She took me through the prayer line, and the pastor and several other church leaders laid hands on me and prayed for my healing. Within a few days the patches of eczema on my skin were completely gone. There were no scars, and I never had another outbreak.

No matter how big or minuscule your own faith may be, you can begin to trust God for His healing, peace, and guidance. And in the process, your faith and trust can mature as you embrace His promises and provisions for you, His child. Too often we tend to sigh and say, "Well, now all we can do is pray. The doctors have done all they know to do."

Yet when healing is needed, prayer should be our first priority. In any crisis, the first words on our lips should be to invite the power of the Lord to invade our situation! He wants to heal us body, mind, and soul.

In this book we will encourage you to do the following:

- Explore God's promises for healing

- Discover prayers you can pray based on biblical principles

- Experience God's peace in the midst of your uncertainties

- Learn to depend on God, knowing without a doubt that He will never leave or forsake you

- Seek the Holy Spirit's guidance for the decisions you'll have to make

- Learn to pray not only for your healing, but also for the healing of others

- Move from an attitude of hopelessness to one infused with faith despite your pain

We pray these stories, scriptures, and prayers will strengthen you to believe that God, our *Jehovah Rophe*, still heals. May God help us to remember that it's our business to pray, and it's His business to heal. Let's tap into His healing power today!

—QUIN SHERRER AND RUTHANNE GARLOCK

...The Cross of Christ has opened a door to healing as part of salvation's provision. Healing encompasses God's power to restore broken hearts, broken homes, broken lives, and broken bodies. Suffering assumes a multiplicity of forms, but Christ's blood not only covers our sin with redemptive love; His stripes release a resource of healing at every dimension of our need.[1]

—*Jack W. Hayford*

1

Lord,
I NEED YOUR HELP

Surely He has borne our griefs
And carried our sorrows;
Yet we esteemed Him stricken,
Smitten by God, and afflicted.
But He was wounded for our transgressions,
He was bruised for our iniquities;
The chastisement for our peace was upon Him,
And by His stripes we are healed.

—ISAIAH 53:4–5

AGGRESSIVE LEUKEMIA. PERSISTENT pain. Incurable injuries. "Lord, I need Your help" was the cry of people with these immobilizing situations. All are completely well today, and you will meet them in this chapter.

The above Scripture verses refer to Christ's sacrifice not only for our salvation, but also for our healing: "…He has borne our griefs and carried our sorrows…." The words for *griefs* and *sorrows* in the original Hebrew specifically mean "physical affliction";

1

the words *borne* and *carried* refer to what He accomplished on the cross.[2]

God heals by many means: through anointing with oil and the prayer of faith, through laying on of hands, through declaring the Word of God, through medical treatment, through the body's natural recuperative powers, and yes, through miracles—sometimes instantaneous, sometimes progressive.

Perhaps you've recently received a bad report from your medical test, or a loved one has just suffered a serious injury. The stunning blow of such news instantly turns your world upside down. But now is the time to lift up your shield of faith and determine to draw strength from God's Word. Remember, the doctors' prognosis is not always the final answer!

Healing was a trademark of Jesus' earthly ministry and also of the early church. Luke says of Jesus, "The news about him spread all the more, so that crowds of people came to hear him and to be healed of their sicknesses" (Luke 5:15, NIV). Throughout the four Gospels we read that He healed deafness, leprosy, blindness, palsy, spinal disorders, mental illness, hemorrhaging and fevers, and terminal illnesses. He even raised the dead.

Jehovah Rophe

> God anointed Jesus of Nazareth with the Holy Spirit and with power, who went about doing good and healing all who were oppressed by the devil, for God was with him.
>
> —ACTS 10:38

I am the God who heals thee

Nowhere does Scripture teach that divine healing ended when the last apostle died, as some people believe. After the Resurrection, when He gave the Great Commission, Jesus said, "And these signs will follow those who believe: In My name...they will lay hands on the sick, and they will recover" (Mark 16:17–18). The only requirement is to be a believer.

SURPRISED BY HEALING

I (Quin) learned this truth in a dramatic way a long time ago. The year was 1972. I was visiting a small prayer group composed of folks from the church my mom had started attending after she'd retired to Destin, Florida. My old-line denominational beliefs were to be shattered that night.

A phone call interrupted the prayer meeting with news that Bill, a thirty-one-year-old Air Force veterinarian who had been diagnosed with acute leukemia, was not expected to live through the weekend. The group immediately began crying out for God to intervene.

"Count me out, Lord," I mouthed silently as the others prayed. "I don't know if You still heal today, so hear their prayers, not mine." I really was puzzled. I'd always been taught that healing miracles ceased with the New Testament church. But the people gathered in this living room were praying with such boldness and faith.

While various ones prayed, one man shocked me when he shouted loudly, "Satan, we give you notice that you and your demonic forces cannot have Bill Lance. He is God's property, and we are standing in the gap for his complete healing. Spirits of infirmity, leave him, in Jesus' name." I had never heard anyone address the devil before, but he spoke with great authority and assurance.

These people truly believe that Bill is going to be healed, I thought to myself as I buried my head in my hands. A few weeks earlier, these folks had held a special healing service for him, with many in the small Florida fishing community coming to pray as Bill knelt at the altar and his pastor, Forrest Mobley, and a group of elders laid

3

hands on him. But here I was, an outsider who was unsure about the whole idea of healing, looking in on faith for the first time.

The hostess saw my questioning look and explained that chemotherapy was not reducing the cancer. Instead it was causing Bill's body to experience hemorrhaging, pain, and anemia. The doctors had said he had the worst form of leukemia, with the bone marrow mass-producing cancerous blood cells too rapidly for the treatment to be effective. Now they believed he had reached the end of his fight. But these people continued praying with great confidence, as though they didn't even hear the doctors' grim report.

Late that same night, in his hospital room in Mississippi, Bill and his wife, Sharon, held hands and repeated the Lord's Prayer, as they did each night. But now something significant happened.

Tears suddenly began cascading down Bill's cheeks. Sobs convulsed him. He felt fire, like a charge of light, shooting through his body. Somehow he knew the presence of Jesus had filled the room. He couldn't even explain to Sharon what he had just experienced.

The next morning, when doctors examined a bone marrow sample from his chest, it showed no sign of cancerous cells. In fact, it was normal. Bill believed the hot light he felt penetrating his body the night before was God's healing touch, flooding him through and through.

When I met and interviewed a healthy Bill the next summer, I had already begun a faith search of my own, poring over Bible passages on healing. In the years since I have interviewed many others who also have received God's healing intervention in their lives.

After more than thirty years, I am happy to report that Bill is still well and very active. For some twenty years he has been at the helm of a company that specializes in developing pharmaceuticals that are used to address the needs of wildlife specialists in safari parks, zoos, state and national parks, and research institutions around the globe. He was just back from Africa when we talked on the phone recently. It's not unusual for him to be called to various parts of the world to help in disease-testing or in administering safe drugs to rhinos, elephants, or other wildlife.

"My career allows me to follow my passion and live a blessed life," he told me.

Bill has also cofounded a company that focuses on developing new drug delivery technologies to improve human health. God certainly had a full and exciting life planned for this man when He reached down and saved Bill from leukemia in that military hospital! Today Bill enjoys having his children and grandchildren living near him in their Colorado home, and he and Sharon continue to be involved in church activities.

"Doctors once told me that leukemia is never healed—only that patients sometimes have a remission," he said. "The form of leukemia I had rarely goes into remission, but I believe that Jesus Christ is the Great Physician." After all these years, doctors have finally agreed that Bill is healed. Whenever opportunities arise, he shares his personal story of healing.[3]

As for me, I no longer doubt that Jesus is our Healer. True, not everyone who prays for healing is healed. I don't for a second believe that those who aren't healed lack the necessary faith for healing. But I do believe we often miss the healing God intends because we don't pray persistently for His strong intervention on our behalf. I have beside my bed a Scripture plaque that reads, "Nothing is impossible with God."

When a healing miracle occurs, others are touched with His awesome power, too. Just hearing that someone has been healed increases our faith. As mentioned earlier, healing can come by many different means. But always we acknowledge God's handiwork in restoring a body.

Jehovah Rophe

> Praise the LORD, O my soul,
>   and forget not all his benefits—
> who forgives all your sins
>   and heals all your diseases...
> who satisfies your desires with good things
>   so that your youth is renewed like the eagle's.
>   —PSALM 103:2–3, 5, NIV

I am the God who heals thee

Our next story is about an accident victim who desperately needed God's healing intervention when all medical solutions had failed. An inspired sermon was the means of igniting her faith.

CALL OUT, CRY OUT

Beverly Hilliard had suffered from severe back pain for three years after a speeding SUV ran a red light and hit her car head-on. Her car was demolished. Her two-year-old son was injured so badly he had to undergo plastic surgery, but he did have a full recovery.

She herself was on pain medication, but nothing could take away her constant backache, making it difficult for her to walk up a flight of stairs, let alone bend down to pick up anything. Fourteen weeks of physical therapy didn't alleviate the pain, nor did the injections and numerous treatments her doctors administered to her spine.

A friend invited Beverly to a women's prayer gathering to listen to the taped message that Pastor Dutch Sheets had delivered at a women's conference a few weeks earlier. "I'm going, and I believe God is going to heal me tonight," she told her husband.

That evening she joined thirty women gathered in a home in

her small Tennessee town to listen to the sermon on crying out to God.

The text was Jeremiah 33:3: "Call to Me and I will answer you and show you great and mighty things, fenced in and hidden, which you do not know..." (AMP). In this instance "to call" means "to cry, to summon, or proclaim" unto the Lord.[4]

As Pastor Sheets got into the heart of his message, he declared:

> This is the year of great deliverance. God is going to show up. We are about to receive what we have been asking for for a long time—this is the season of breakthrough. We call for power evangelism with signs, wonders and miracles.
>
> Now is the time to speak to the mountain to be removed. Now is the time to war in a different way. Begin to use your voice like a weapon and speak forth. This is the time to apply Jeremiah 33:3.

His words of encouragement released a bolt of faith like a charge of electricity that touched everyone in the room. Each woman received a different key, a different dose of faith, so to speak. Then they began praying for one another.

All of a sudden Beverly was touched by the power of God—her pain was gone! She was instantly healed.

When she got home that evening, her husband immediately noticed the difference in her and began rejoicing and praising God. Beverly stopped taking her medication and returned to work.

What had happened? The Word of God, proclaimed by an anointed preacher, had released faith in the listeners to believe for signs, wonders, and miracles. Then they did something about it. They called out to God, and He answered. Beverly had gone to the meeting with a high faith level, expecting to receive her healing. The message released that faith, and prayers by ordinary women

touched the throne room of an extraordinary God.
Call out. Cry out. Believe He will answer!

Jehovah Rophe

> "Hear, O LORD, and be merciful to me;
>   O LORD, be my help."
> You turned my wailing into dancing;
>   you removed my sackcloth and clothed me with joy,
> that my heart may sing to you and not be silent.
>   O LORD my God, I will give you thanks forever.
> —PSALM 30:10–12, NIV

I am the God who heals thee

MEDITATE, MEMORIZE, AND SAY ALOUD

Have you ever found yourself meditating on certain Scripture verses over and over? You were hiding the Word of God in your heart much like depositing great treasure in a bank, even though you didn't realize it at the time.

The psalmist declares that a person who meditates on the law (God's Word) day and night is "like a tree planted by streams of water, which yields its fruit in season and whose leaf does not wither. Whatever he does prospers" (Ps. 1:3, NIV). In Hebrew, the word for *meditate* (v. 2) means to "ponder, mutter, speak, or study."[5]

Meditating on Scripture like this equips you so that in a time of crisis the Word of God can flow from your mouth with boldness.

Kim and Rusty's family lived through this in a practical way after attending a convention in Fort Worth more than ten years ago. "We came away with a new revelation," Kim reported. "We learned that we have benefits because we are in covenant with Almighty God!"

After returning home, Kim had been looking up scriptures on God's covenants with His people, and also verses that tell how Satan gets confused and confounded, then falls into the net or trap that he lays for us. (See Psalm 35:7–8.)

One verse she had found and meditated on a lot refers to the enemies of God's people: "They intended evil against You; they devised a plot which they are not able to perform" (Ps. 21:11).

Little did Kim know that God's Word, mixed with faith, would yield miraculous results in the life of her son John. When a teenage driver lost control of his car and hit her ten-year-old, almost totally severing his leg, Kim found herself declaring Bible verses that just popped into her mind in the midst of the crisis.

If you were to see John today you would agree he is a walking miracle. This 285-pound, 6-foot-2-inch guy played defensive lineman on the Samford University football team his first two years there. Now in his third year of college, he's retired from football. His mother tells the story:

September 14, 1995, was a warm sunny day in our Alabama community when I left our house to go pick up my three oldest children from school. On our return, as I pulled into our driveway, I asked my second-oldest son John to cross the street and get the mail from the mailbox. The other two boys wiggled out of the car around the baby's car seat and followed him. Because my van was facing away from the road and was on a slight incline I could not see the children. But I soon heard the sound of a fast-approaching car, then the screeching of tires, a horrible thud, a crash, the breaking of glass, then the screams of my children.

Instead of panic, a righteous anger rose up in me. *How dare*

Satan attack someone who has a covenant with Almighty God! I thought. Then I heard myself scream, "The adversary has great evil plans and devises a plot, but he can't perform it!" Satan's plan was to kill or maim John, devastate us, and ruin the life of the young driver if he committed vehicular homicide.

As I jumped from my van the Holy Spirit gave me my first instruction—in order to walk in the faith I needed, I must walk in love by not being angry at whoever had hurt my child. I replied, "Yes, Sir." Right then I chose to forgive.

I later learned that when the teenage driver saw John on the side of the road, he braked suddenly and lost control of the car, slamming right into him. The impact caused my son to hit the windshield and go flying onto the road, where he suffered multiple injuries.

Racing toward John, who was lying in a bloody, mangled heap about fifty feet from me, I began to scream the Word of God. "You 'shall not die, but live, and declare the works of the LORD'" (Ps. 118:17). Then I uttered a prayer, "O Lord, let him live!"

His left leg was lying at a strange angle away from his body over his head, severed except for a small piece of skin. Bones were exposed in his elbows. The skin on his left cheek was peeled away, and his left ear was dangling. A large laceration between his eyes caused blood to pool in his eyes. Deep gashes were all over his body.

"Momma, I wasn't in the road—why did he hit me?" he said.

The Holy Spirit quickened my next thoughts and words, reminding me of the story of the Shunammite woman in 2 Kings 4. Even though her son was dead, she said, "It is well" (v. 26). So I said very emphatically, "John, all is well."

I laid my hands on him and spoke again, "You shall not die, but live." Then I had him repeat after me, "I shall not die, but live... I'm healed by the stripes of Jesus." (See Psalm 118:17; 1 Peter 2:24.) As soon as he said those words he lapsed into unconsciousness.

I continued to pray in the Spirit and to declare the promises that the Lord brought to my mind. One was Romans 8:11: "But if the Spirit of Him who raised Jesus from the dead dwells in you, He who raised Christ from the dead will also give life to your mortal bodies…."

As a trained nurse I could evaluate the situation better than most. I saw that my son was hemorrhaging badly, so I prayed for the bleeding to stop and commanded him to live. (See Ezekiel 16:6.)

I believe that because we are God's creation, we can take authority over all the works of God's hands (Ps. 8:6). Since John's body was one of those works, I took authority over head injuries and commanded, in the name of Jesus, for the brain not to swell. I spoke to the respiratory and circulatory systems and commanded all internal organs to be whole and to function normally. His abdomen was distended, indicating internal bleeding. It was obvious that his leg was broken—a more accurate term was "broken off" except for a small piece of skin twisted around and around.

As I prayed over his left leg, I began quoting Psalm 34:20: "He guards all his bones, not one of them is broken." At the time I felt rather silly saying those words because there were broken bones sticking out in every direction. But faith rose up in me. I untwisted John's leg and aligned his body on the road while crying out to God to send help.

Immediately a car pulled up. The driver used his cell phone to call 9-1-1 and then my husband. The second car to stop was driven by a home-health nurse who had medical supplies. She made a tourniquet for John's leg. She said his brain was exposed, so she pressurized the head wound with gauze.

Police and paramedics arrived within four minutes after receiving the call. I knew we were in a fight for my son's life, and my role was prayer—which at that moment was more important than any of the first aid I could remember from my nurse's training.

As soon as my husband, Rusty, arrived, he also began speaking the Word of God over John's neck, back, and spinal cord injuries. Because of John's massive blood loss—over half of his blood volume—the paramedics were unable to start an IV, so they immediately rushed him to the hospital.

The health nurse who had been administering aid cautioned them about his head injury. As they were immobilizing him, the pressure bandages fell off, and his head wound was already completely closed up. Chalk up the first miracle! They placed a "blow-up-cast" immobilizer over his leg and sped him to the nearby hospital.

During the first minutes at the hospital our pastor was allowed to anoint him with oil and pray over him. He read, "Now may the God of peace Himself sanctify you completely; and may your whole spirit, soul, and body be preserved blameless at the coming of our Lord Jesus Christ. He who calls you is faithful, who also will do it" (1 Thess. 5:23–24).

As he prayed, I touched John's toes and spoke words of healing over his leg. The head nurse standing by me told me he had a pulse in his foot, indicating that there was now blood flow to the foot. Was this miracle number two? I knew we were experiencing a manifestation of healing and the restoring power of God.

Because this happened at school dismissal time, news of the accident spread quickly. The teachers met to pray. Even the football team stopped their practice to pray. Our friends flooded the emergency room to pray.

First in order was to get John stabilized and to evaluate his injuries. The doctors determined most of his injuries were on the left side, and his vital signs were not great. His left collarbone, several ribs, and both bones in the arms were broken. There were multiple breaks in his pelvis. The most obvious injury was to his leg, which was a grade 3 trauma—the worst kind. His whole body was skinned. He was badly bruised. His eyes were swollen shut, and he was unrecognizable.

A doctor friend who went in to see him came out crying. "I'm so sorry…," he told me as he wept. I took him by his collar and firmly said, "He shall live and not die! He is healed by the stripes of Jesus, and no weapon formed against him will prosper!"

My friend was not offended, but I knew I had to watch my

confession and not repeat to others the severity of John's injuries or the improbability of his survival. I couldn't let fear or doubt rule, nor could I allow negative words to come from my mouth. Yet I had to say things that would be socially acceptable to my friends and relatives.

Suddenly, I remembered that the previous summer John had given all of his vacation money to a missionary headed to China. God reminded me of the promise in Psalm 41:1–2: "How blessed is he who considers the helpless; the LORD will deliver him in a day of trouble. The LORD will protect him, and keep him alive…" (NAS). To me that meant that because of John's compassion on the spiritually helpless, he had a covenant with God and had promises working for him.

I shared this little anecdote with our friends to block out doubt and unbelief, and to keep me from having to relive the horrors of the accident. I could retell the story of John's actions last summer and quote the Word, which brought others into agreement with me. And it established an atmosphere of faith around all of us.

The doctors determined that John had no internal injuries or bleeding, so he was taken to surgery to have the broken bones set. Not only was the leg broken, but also because large chunks were missing, the bones did not fit back together correctly. They placed metal rods outside his body and left the leg open to drain for several days, allowing them to determine what soft tissue was not receiving blood and oxygen.

Three days later when he went back to surgery to remove dead tissue, they found that none had died. They cleaned the wound, closed up the leg, and attached a metal rod to the outside of John's body holding the leg on.

The first night after the accident, John's symptoms indicated that the broken ribs had punctured a lung. We prayed over his respiratory system and with authority paraphrased Acts 17:25, "He Himself gives all men life and breath." His acute symptoms stopped, and they canceled the preparations to fly him to another hospital.

After a week John was moved from intensive care, and after

the second week, he was sent home to mend. The doctors were constantly excited at his rapid rate of recovery.

While we had some immediate miracles, we had to wait for healing in other areas. At first the medical team gave us no hope that he would live. Then there was no guarantee that he would keep his badly injured leg. Finally, when it was clear that his leg had been saved, they said he wouldn't walk or run. Over time, he did all these things.

After being released from the hospital, John continued to improve at home, where he completed the fourth grade with a teacher who came to the house. His head injury did not cause him to lag behind scholastically. He was anemic due to all the broken bones, and since that affects one's immune system, the doctors didn't want him around other people. We claimed the promise in Psalm 91:10 that no plague would come near his dwelling, and he never became sick.

We believed God wanted him fully restored without scarring. We prayed that John would be a youth "without blemish, well-favored in appearance and skillful in all wisdom…" and that his life would be redeemed from the pit—beautified and dignified. (See Daniel 1:4; Psalm 103:4, AMP.)

Within a few months John was up and running and playing baseball. The policeman who had been on the scene at John's accident came to his first game. He looked us up in the crowd and, with tears in his eyes, told us he marveled at how John could possibly be playing ball.

We moved to Birmingham when John was in the eighth grade, and he was recruited to play football. His jersey number was 50—for Jubilee, meaning the restoration of all things. To those who didn't know what had happened, John was just a team player. But to his family, it meant a lot to see number 50 running up and down the field so fast on a God-restored leg.

His high school football team won the 5-A state championship his senior year, and he was named the most valuable defensive player for his team. Academically, he ranked in the upper 1 percent in the nation. As part of God's restoration for him, John was awarded a football scholarship to Samford University, where he wanted to go.

The lessons our family learned through this experience continue to influence our reactions and decisions in our faith walk on a daily basis.

FINDING STRENGTH IN SCRIPTURE

Kim remembers that when the doctors asked her which specialists she wanted called in, she thought to herself, *It doesn't matter, because the Lord is the real Physician in this case.* And indeed He was.

Some might say that she simply was in denial regarding her son's critical condition because she refused to speak of his injuries. But when she shared her story with us, it was clear that she knew all too well that John's life was hanging in the balance, literally. She simply believed that God in His providence had prepared her and Rusty by causing them to store Scripture in their hearts. They chose to obey the Holy Spirit's leading and stay focused on the Word.

Jehovah Rophe

> O LORD my God, I called to you for help
>   and you healed me.
> O LORD, you brought me up from the grave;
>   you spared me from going down into the pit.
>   —PSALM 30:2–3, NIV

I am the God who heals thee

Obviously, Kim and her husband were better prepared for the crisis than they realized. As they declared scriptures over their son, the Word created an atmosphere of faith throughout John's journey back to wholeness. And they were blessed with praying friends and relatives and good doctors and pastors who stood with them.

Of course, many families face similar crises without such a strong foundation of faith in the Scripture and a network of praying friends. If you need a boost in your own faith and understanding of God's Word regarding healing, we trust you will find a remedy in this book. In our next chapter, we'll discuss the matter of asking God to increase our faith.

PRAYING GOD'S PROMISES

Following are paraphrased Scripture prayers that you can use as a guideline for composing your own Scripture prayers to suit your circumstances.

PRAYER

Dear Jesus, I acknowledge You as my Lord and Savior. Thank You that You took away my sins when You died on the cross. You knew me even before I was born, and You have a plan for my life. (See John 3:16; Psalm 139:13–16; Ephesians 2:10.)

Father God, in the name of Jesus, I come to You humbly, yet boldly, basing my prayer on Your Word to declare that by Jesus' stripes I can appropriate Christ's healing. Lord, I pray, renew my health in every area of my body. (See Isaiah 53:13–14; 1 Peter 2:24.)

O God, I know nothing is impossible for You. When Jesus lived on this earth He went throughout the land healing disease and sickness among the people. Because Your Word declares that Jesus Christ is the same yesterday, today, and forever, I know You still heal today. Thank You that Your healing power is working in me. (See Luke 1:37; Matthew 4:23; Hebrews 13:8.)

Lord, please restore _____ (insert name) to complete wholeness. I praise You that You are a God of power, the Creator God who knows us so intimately. I trust You to touch _____ (insert name) now, O gentle Savior. Amen.

The thing above all else I want you to see is that you cannot generate [faith]; you cannot work it up; you cannot manufacture it. It is imparted and infused by God Himself. You cannot...turn your hope and desire into faith by your own power. The only place you can get it is from the Lord, for the Word clearly and distinctly states that faith is one of two things. It is either a gift of God, or it is a fruit of the Spirit.[1]

—*Charles S. Price*

2

Lord,
INCREASE MY FAITH

> "...If you [Jesus] can do anything, take pity on us and help us."
>
> "'If you can'?" said Jesus. "Everything is possible for him who believes."
>
> Immediately the boy's father exclaimed, "I do believe; help me overcome my unbelief!"
>
> —MARK 9:22–24, NIV

PROBABLY ALL OF us are a mixture of faith and doubt, just as the father in the above story obviously was when he appealed to Jesus for help. Most Christians have no problem believing that God *can* heal. The challenge is to activate our faith to believe God *will* heal in a specific situation we're concerned about. It's unlikely that in this life we will ever be able to say our faith is perfect. But based on this passage in the Gospel of Mark, there is absolutely nothing wrong with asking God to increase our faith.

When this father brought his son to the disciples and asked them to drive the spirit out of the boy, they could not. But then Jesus came on the scene, and the father appealed to Him to do something about the seizures that had plagued his son since childhood. Upon seeing Jesus, the evil spirit threw the boy into a convulsion, causing him to roll on the ground and foam at the mouth.

Jesus assured the father, "All things can be (are possible) to him who believes!" This prompted the man to respond, "Lord, I believe! [Constantly] help my weakness of faith!" (Mark 9:23–24, AMP).

When Jesus rebuked the evil spirit it shrieked, convulsed the boy violently, and came out, leaving him motionless on the ground. Those in the crowd thought the boy was dead, but after Jesus took him by the hand and lifted him to his feet, he stood up—obviously healed.

Even though the father's faith was lacking, Jesus responded to his appeal and healed the man's son. God does not require that our faith be perfect. But He does want us to act on the faith we do have and to be honest enough to ask that He increase our faith.

Jehovah Rophe

Therefore, since we have a great high priest who has gone through the heavens, Jesus the Son of God, let us hold firmly to the faith we profess. For we do not have a high priest who is unable to sympathize with our weaknesses, but we have one who has been tempted in every way, just as we are—yet was without sin. Let us then approach the throne of grace with confidence, so that we may receive mercy and find grace to help us in our time of need.

—HEBREWS 4:14–16, NIV

I am the God who heals thee

As we learned in the last chapter, the more we meditate on the Word of God, the more we will see our faith level rise. Scripture tells us, "Faith comes by hearing, and hearing by the word of God" (Rom. 10:17).

Our longtime friend Beth Alves discovered the power of acting on the Word of God to receive healing in a surprising way, as you will see in the next story.

TESTING THE WORD OF GOD

During Beth and Floyd Alves's family vacation late one summer, twelve-year-old Julee was ill much of the time. After they returned home, they discovered she was unable to swallow, so she was admitted to the hospital for a series of tests. Over the next several weeks she was in and out of the hospital numerous times.

Finally, the doctor gave his diagnosis: Julee had a brain tumor, and he was not yet sure whether surgery would be possible. Upon hearing that report, Floyd wept. But Beth immediately said, "She will live and not die, and see the salvation of the Lord.

"I had no idea I was declaring the truth from Psalm 118:17," she told us. "I didn't read the Bible on a regular basis, but every Sunday the reading of Scripture was a part of our liturgy, so I must have heard that psalm read in church. The doctor thought I was in denial about how serious the situation was, so he sent a psychologist to talk to me several times. Each time I told her the same thing I had declared to the doctor."

During the next several weeks, Beth stayed with Julee almost continually. Often as she walked the halls of the hospital she would repeat the phrases, "Jesus Christ is the same yesterday, today, and forever" (Heb. 13:8), and "She will live and not die, and see the salvation of the Lord."

"I never doubted that God could heal," she recalled. "But it was never mentioned in my church, and I didn't know anyone who had been healed. I'd always been told that God was too busy running the universe to be bothered with our relatively minor problems. I remember weeping and wishing that I lived in Jesus' day so that I could go to Him and ask Him to heal my daughter, and I knew He would."

Julee came home from the hospital for Christmas that year, but by New Year's Day she was unable to walk or talk. Beth took her back to the doctor, who sent her to the children's terminal ward of a much larger hospital. Now Beth knew beyond any doubt that Julee's condition was critical.

The doctor ordered one more test to determine for sure whether or not they could remove the tumor. On the night before the test, Beth was in the room with Julee as she slept, and she was looking for something special to read. Finding a Bible in the drawer of the nightstand, she just happened to open it to Mark 16 and read verses 17–18 (KJV):

> And these signs shall follow them that believe; In my name shall they cast out devils; they shall speak with new tongues; they shall take up serpents; and if they drink any deadly thing, it shall not hurt them; they shall lay hands on the sick, and they shall recover.

"The last phrase of that verse stood out to me, and I just decided to do what the Scripture said," she reported. "I didn't feel any sudden surge of faith, and in fact, I didn't even pray. With the Bible open to that passage, I put it across Julee's ankles, laid hands on her by taking hold of her feet, then declared, 'God, I'm doing it!' I put the Bible back in the drawer and stayed in the room the rest of the night."

Jehovah Rophe

> The apostles said to the Lord, "Increase our faith!" He replied, "If you have faith as small as a mustard seed, you can say to this mulberry tree, 'Be uprooted and planted in the sea,' and it will obey you."
>
> —Luke 17:5–6, niv

I am the God who heals thee

The next morning, after the test was finished, the doctor came out to the waiting area with tears in his eyes and said to Beth, "I'll see you back in Julee's room."

Fearing that Julee had died during the test, Beth went back to the room to wait. She was sitting with her head in her hands, staring at the puddle her tears had made on the floor, when the orderlies wheeled Julee into the room. Suddenly the distraught mom heard her daughter talking.

"Where's my daddy?" Julee asked. "I'm hungry—let's eat!"

"She had not been able to talk for days," Beth said. "And before that, she didn't even recognize Floyd when he came to see her. It was an astounding miracle! The doctor walked in while Julee was still talking and had to admit that something amazing had happened."

Today Julee is a busy pastor's wife with four sons and no residual effects from the tumor. In the years since, Beth and Floyd have experienced the infilling of the Holy Spirit and have seen many healings occur in response to prayer. Also, they have established Increase International, a multifaceted prayer ministry based in Bulverde, Texas.*

---

* Based on personal interview with Beth Alves on June 20, 2005. For more information on her ministry, go to http://www.increaseinternational.org.

How Does God Heal?

Since everyone's faith is not the same, God sovereignly deals with us in various ways. However, we must be careful not to box God in, presuming He will answer in our preconceived way or time frame. As we grow in our relationship with Him, we can more clearly discern the difference between presumption and faith. After all, our faith is in God, not just in our expected miracle.

Throughout the book we will discuss in more detail some of the ways God heals. But for starters, let's summarize them.

- Through people with the "gifts of healings" (1 Cor. 12:9) or by "extraordinary miracles" as He did in Ephesus through Paul (Acts 19:11–12): Today, thousands are drawn to crusades where anointed men and women of God with the gift of healing pray for miracles.

- Through "laying on of hands" the sick are made well (Mark 16:18). (See Hebrews 6:1–2.)

- Through speaking God's Word: "My word...shall not return to Me void, but it shall accomplish what I please..." (Isa. 55:11). (See Mark 11:23; 2 Corinthians 4:13; Matthew 7:7; Hebrews 4:12.)

- Through asking in the name of Jesus: "I will do whatever you ask in my name, so that the Son may bring glory to the Father" (John 14:13, NIV). (See John 16:23; Acts 3:1–8.)

- Through anointing with oil and the prayer of faith (James 5:14–16; Mark 6:13)

- Through believing you receive when you pray (Mark 11:24)

- Through confessing of sins and receiving Holy Communion with faith (1 Cor. 11:23–32)

- Through two or more agreeing in prayer (Matt. 18:19–20)

- Declaring or appropriating the blood covenant—Christ, the sacrificial lamb whose body was broken for us, His blood shed for us (See 1 Corinthians 11:23–32; Exodus 12:1–13.)

- Through anointed cloths: God performed miracles through Paul when "handkerchiefs and aprons that had touched him were taken to the sick, and their illnesses were cured…" (Acts 19:12, NIV). Evangelist Smith Wigglesworth (1851–1947), who likened them to a "storage battery," sent anointed cloths to people with all kinds of illnesses and received hundreds of reports of healing and deliverance.

The primary secret of Wigglesworth's remarkable ministry of healing was his absolute faith in God's Word. His advice was:

> Believers are strong only as the Word of God abides in them. The Word of God is spirit and life to those who receive it in simple faith….Know your Book, live it, believe it, and obey it. Hide God's Word in your heart. It will save your soul, quicken your body, and illumine your mind….Inactivity of faith is a robber which steals blessing. Increase comes by action, by using what we have and what we know.[2]

The couple in our next story took action on what they knew, limited as it was. But their knowledge and faith grew by leaps and bounds, leading to incredible answers to prayer.

Could God Heal Their Baby?

Jessica and Tim White needed increased faith that God could heal their son, though they attended a church that didn't acknowledge that God still heals today. The morning after John Nicholas was born, a nurse saw that he was on the verge of dying from a lack of oxygen. She quickly alerted his pediatrician, who happened to be in the hospital at the time.

Doctors soon discovered he had a congenital heart disease known as "transposition of the great vessels"—meaning his pulmonary and aorta were connected in reverse positions. The doctors were able to stabilize the baby enough to make the ambulance trip to Memphis, accompanied by a neonatal specialist and a nurse. John Nicholas was only six days old when he had his first operation.

At age six months he had emergency surgery to remove scar tissue and the faulty pulmonary valve. The surgeons enlarged his pulmonary artery, then stitched it up so that it opened and closed "like a fish mouth," they explained.

Jehovah Rophe

By his power God raised the Lord from the dead, and he will raise us also. Do you not know that your bodies are members of Christ himself?

—1 Corinthians 6:14–15, NIV

I am the God who heals thee

Four years later, in his third operation, doctors used the jugular vein of a cow to give John Nicholas a new pulmonary artery and valve—a risky procedure requiring special permission. But the following year, when complications arose with the new valve, doctors did a heart catheterization and inserted a stent to help his heart function normally. After a seemingly endless wait, the parents finally got the bad news. "I don't know what to tell you," the surgeon said, "but the valve we put in last year is messed up."

That "cow valve" should have lasted for ten years to see their son through normal childhood. But now, when he's only five years old, they learn that this solution isn't working the way they had hoped. The doctor told them to bring John Nicholas back to the hospital three months later when they would decide what to do.

About six months before receiving this report, Tim and Jessica had begun attending a church where they heard for the first time a full gospel message, including the news that Jesus still heals. They studied for themselves many passages in the Bible pertaining to healing and miracles. When I (Quin) spoke for their church's women's retreat, I mentioned the need for the baptism of the Holy Spirit—something entirely new to them. Jessica said she was open to receive all that God had for her.

One day while all alone in her bedroom, Jessica prayed to be baptized in the Holy Spirit. Suddenly aware of the overwhelming presence of God, she fell to the floor and began speaking in tongues. After this amazing encounter she crawled up off the floor, went to her son's room, laid hands on him, and then began praying in the new language she had just received. The whole incident seemed unreal at the time, but she knew the power of the Holy Spirit was working through her.

"I didn't really know what I was doing, but I had new faith—faith to believe God for healing," she said. "Tim and I began praying differently. Instead of begging God to heal, we began to thank God and declare in our prayers that by Jesus' stripes our son had been healed."

Three weeks after her experience with the Holy Spirit, Jessica was sitting in a restaurant talking to her friend Lisa when a young man and his companion joined them at their table. They listened intently as Jessica told about John Nicholas's appointment coming up the following week, and also about the vision problems he'd had for a couple of years. Though she was believing for God's healing, she still wondered what the doctors would recommend. Lisa's friend became very interested and asked if he could pray for her son right then, sitting in the restaurant. It was a powerful, faith-packed prayer, proclaiming that the Lord, the great Creator, was healing the little boy's heart as well as his eyes. The four of them prayed in agreement for John Nicholas's complete healing.

A week later Tim and Jessica were back in Memphis for their son's evaluation. After the tests were finished, the cardiologist finally appeared with prints from the echocardiogram to give them his report. He looked at the prints, then hurriedly left the room. "I thought I had the wrong pictures," he explained when he came back. "I have never seen this child's heart look this good. It is the size and shape it is supposed to be. I can't believe it! He looks great. Sounds good."

The doctor was so pleased he told Tim and Jessica they didn't need to bring John Nicholas back for six months. To go that long before another medical appointment seemed incredible to Jessica. God had answered their prayers! They were confident that God had completely healed their son's heart problems.

But a new surprise awaited them after they got back from the doctor's office. Tim left for a men's retreat (where he would be baptized in the Holy Spirit), while Jessica and John Nicholas joined some women and children from church for a covered-dish supper. The kids were running and playing inside and out while the women visited.

Suddenly John Nicholas ran up to his mother in the kitchen and handed her his glasses. "Here, Mom; I don't need these glasses anymore—I can see without them," he said. And he hasn't worn glasses since.

At the next heart evaluation, the doctor listened to the boy's heart and said he saw no need to do further testing. "At your next appointment in six months, we'll do a high-image CT scan as a baseline for future treatment," he told the ecstatic parents.

It was a big letdown six months later when that CT scan revealed two areas of narrowing in his pulmonary artery, which the doctors proposed to repair through heart catheterization and inserting a stent.

"Before the surgery, fourteen people gathered to anoint John Nicholas with oil and pray for the restoration of his healing," his mother reported. After the procedure the report was astounding beyond their expectations. What the scan showed was only a minor narrowing in one area. In fact, they didn't even install the stent because it wasn't needed.

"You don't understand—that CT scanner has never been wrong before," the surgeon told the parents as he drew a picture of the difference between what the scan had shown and what he had discovered during the procedure.

Jessica and Tim continue to tell their son's miracle story to anyone who will listen. John Nicholas takes no medications, not even aspirin. He will only see his doctor at six-month intervals. A few months ago when he had to have tests done for another matter, they also checked his heart because of his medical history. The cardiologist who read the report said he couldn't even tell John Nicholas had ever had a heart problem. The faith adventure of this family illustrates the truth presented by Bible teacher Graham Cooke:

> When we know what [God] is really like, when our hearts are emboldened by the majesty of His faithfulness and grace, then we know that His commitment to His Word and His

people cannot be broken. His Word will not return to Him empty.... There is always a dimension where faith is beyond our experience. Faith is exploring, pushing us beyond the boundaries of what we know in the natural. As we get used to that faith level, our experience pushes up to it and our faith ranges out further into the heart of God.[3]

Some Christians are further along in their walk of faith than others. As you will see, the woman in our next story operated at an incredible level of faith.

IN NEED OF GOD'S PROTECTION

Karen Clarke needed God's protection one rainy morning as she faced what seemed to be certain death behind the wheel of her car. In her prayer time each day she always asks the Lord to cover her with Jesus' atoning blood. Some people refer to this as "applying the blood of Jesus" for protection and safety. It is based on the Old Testament account of the Israelites when they applied the blood of an unblemished lamb on their doorposts for protection against the destroyer. (See Exodus 12:13, 23.)

Jehovah Rophe

> Now faith is the substance of things hoped for, the evidence of things not seen. For by it the elders obtained a good testimony. By faith we understand that the worlds were framed by the word of God, so that the things which are seen were not made of things which are visible.... But without faith it is impossible to please Him, for he who comes to God must believe that He is, and that He is a rewarder of those who diligently seek Him.
> —HEBREWS 11:1–3, 6

I am the God who heals thee

In the New Testament it was Jesus, the Son of God, who spilled His blood as the unblemished Lamb. When Christians pray by "pleading the blood of Jesus," they are using their spiritual authority, asking in faith for Jesus' protection to cover them. You might say they are praying "preventively" against any forthcoming attack of the enemy.

Karen is convinced that such a prayer saved her life on April 2, 1998, as she was driving in torrential rain from her home in Niceville, Florida, to Pensacola, Florida, to pick up a relative at the airport. She was twenty minutes into her trip when it happened. She tells the story in her own words:

———◆◆◆———

On my way out of town I had stopped by my friend's home where a prayer meeting was in progress and asked for prayer for my trip. Isabel, the leader, kept praying for my neck to be protected. I thought that was a peculiar prayer, but later I realized how important it was. We closed the prayer time by pleading the blood of Jesus over me for this journey.

Driving down the highway in my daughter's brand-new Honda Civic in a blinding rainstorm, I kept thinking I should re-buckle my seatbelt. I had taken it off during a brief stop earlier. But I was afraid to let go of the steering wheel long enough to buckle up. I was praying for everyone else on the road because it was raining so hard. "I plead the blood of Jesus over all of us," I kept saying aloud.

A Dodge Ram truck passed me and then began fishtailing in the pools of water forming on the interstate. It hit a guard rail, spun around, and came right for me, smashing my car head-on. The two vehicles locked together, and we went spinning down the highway. The next thing I knew my car was hit by a loaded semitruck. The impact threw my car in the air, crushing the back of my car and sending it—with me in it—underneath the semi.

Then my car caught fire. But in a strange turn of events, the fire caused the wheels on the semi to blow out, and my car was propelled out from under it. The rain then dowsed the fire. When rescuers arrived at the scene, they had to pry me out.

While en route to the hospital I could hear the attendants tell the hospital over their phone what was wrong with me: "...possible broken neck, head and serious internal injuries." I began saying under my breath, "I cancel that diagnosis in the name of Jesus. The blood of Jesus protects and restores me." I later learned a member of my church was driving by and saw the wreck and began to pray for the family of the people involved because he didn't see how anyone could have survived.

As my head throbbed, I imagined it was like a split watermelon, so I began to bind all the swelling and pain in Jesus' name. Though I couldn't even tell the ambulance attendants my name, I did remember enough to ask them to call Abundant Life Church.

By the time I arrived at the hospital a church elder was there waiting to pray with me. We prayed in agreement, canceling all the negative reports of the doctor. I kept saying, "I command the swelling in my head to go down and for my body to get back in alignment the way God created it. I do this in the name and authority of Jesus, who shed His blood for me."

The state highway patrolman involved in the investigation came to the hospital three times that day just to check on me. He said that in his more than thirty years of patrolling the highways he had never seen a driver survive a wreck that had demolished the car as badly as mine. He told me that if I had been wearing a seatbelt I probably would have been decapitated.

I was dismissed after just one day in the hospital—there were no broken bones, and only the sciatic nerve was bruised. An ophthalmologist who removed the glass particles from my eyes thought it was a miracle that I hadn't suffered damage to my eyesight.

I was sore and limping when I got home, and my husband had

to help me get dressed for the first few days. But I praised God I was alive. Two weeks later I went to an Aglow meeting, and before it began, the guest speaker, whom I didn't know, had "a word of knowledge" for me.

Pointing at me she said, "God says if you will just raise your hands and worship Him, He will heal you." I thought to myself, *She doesn't know that I am hurting so much and can't possibly raise my hands above my waist.* But in obedience I limped over to the piano, and as music played I began to raise my hands in worship. Suddenly, both hands shot up over my head, and all the pain in the sciatic nerve disappeared. I was healed right on the spot! By now I was really singing and worshiping the Lord.

When the company representing the semitruck called to see how much money I wanted for trauma, I told them Jesus was my Healer—that He had completely healed me and I had no trauma. "Keep your money," I said.

Later, when I went to see my wrecked car, it was crushed and burned so severely that the hunk of metal had no resemblance to an automobile. I was wondering whether my Bible had survived the ordeal, when I suddenly spotted it. Because it was surrounded by crushed pieces of metal I couldn't retrieve it, but it was undamaged.

The other drivers involved in the accident? They too survived. I am still convinced that prayers for me and for the other drivers on the rain-splashed road that day helped save our lives—especially applying the blood of Jesus.

You might want to stop right now and pray a prayer like Karen would use daily:

> *Father, I come to You in the name of Jesus, Your Son.*
> *By faith I apply the blood of Jesus over my mind,*
> *my heart, and my body, believing in Your promises*

and the covenant You have established with those who put their trust in You. I choose to align my will with Your will and purpose for my life. Thank You for the protecting power of the blood of Jesus. I give You praise. Amen.

THE HEALING GOD PROVIDES

When Jesus encountered Zacchaeus, the tax collector in Jericho, He declared to him, "For the Son of Man has come to seek and to save that which was lost" (Luke 19:10). But that word *save* promises much more than the English translation implies. In the original text it is the Greek word *sozo*, which also appears as "healed" in some passages. It means, "to save, deliver or protect—also to heal, preserve, or make whole."[4] Clearly, the purpose of Jesus' coming to earth was to minister to the spirit, soul, and body of mankind.

Jehovah Rophe

Christ has redeemed us from the curse of the law, having become a curse for us (for it is written, "Cursed is everyone who hangs on a tree"), that the blessing of Abraham might come upon the Gentiles in Christ Jesus, that we might receive the promise of the Spirit through faith.

—GALATIANS 3:13–14

I am the God who heals thee

One commentator notes that in the eighth chapter of Luke we see a good example of the threefold expression of *sozo*:

- Salvation, or a restored relationship with God through faith, illustrated in the parable of the sower (Luke 8:4–15) when Jesus uses the word *saved* in verse 12.

- Deliverance from demonic powers, based on Jesus delivering a demon-possessed man who, after the demons had departed, was found "sitting at the feet of Jesus, clothed and in his right mind" (Luke 8:26–39).

- Physical healing comes to the woman with the issue of blood when she touches Jesus' garment (Luke 8:43–48). That healing occurred while Jesus was on the way to pray for Jairus's daughter. Upon hearing that the child had died, he said, "Do not be afraid; only believe, and she will be made well" (v. 50)—and then he raised her from the dead (vv. 49–55).[5]

Jesus devoted much of His ministry to healing, and He empowered and encouraged His early followers to do the same.

> When Jesus had called the Twelve together, he gave them power and authority to drive out all demons and to cure diseases, and he sent them out to preach the kingdom of God and to heal the sick.
>
> —LUKE 9:1–2, NIV

Yes, He still heals today and uses those who believe in Him as agents of healing. He declared, "I tell you the truth, anyone who has faith in me will do what I have been doing. He will do even greater things than these, because I am going to the Father" (John 14:12, NIV). Throughout the Bible, God's people are encouraged to pray for healing.

We can establish our faith on the validity of God's Word and His almighty power, even when we cannot understand His ways. Sometimes all we can do is cry out, "Lord, increase my faith!"

PRAYER

Lord Jesus, help me remember Your promise that everything is possible for him who believes. Help me to raise my faith level by focusing on Your Word and spending time in Your presence. Thank You for all the times You have intervened and helped me in the past. According to Your Word I come boldly to Your throne of grace with my petitions. (Name them.) *I praise You for Your steadfast love. Amen.*

Since the day that Christ's blood was shed, since the day of his atonement, he has paid the price to meet all the world's need and its cry of sorrow. Truly Jesus has met the need of the broken hearts and the sorrowful spirits, and also of the withered limbs and the broken bodies. God's dear Son paid the debt for all, for he took our infirmities and bore our sicknesses.[1]

—*Smith Wigglesworth*

3

Lord,
IT HURTS

And He [Jesus] began to teach them that the Son of Man must suffer many things, and be rejected by the elders and chief priests and scribes, and be killed, and after three days rise again.

—MARK 8:31

LORD, IT HURTS! Oh, it hurts so bad," you cry. Whether you have a nagging headache, a broken toe, or a knee sprain, your whole body seems out of sorts. You feel so incapacitated by the pain that your everyday routine is disrupted.

Often it's these small annoyances in life that trouble us and try to steal our health.

Mary Beth Pichotta had to cope with a lot of stress in her usual routine when she gave birth to premature twins while also caring for an eighteen-month-old. Naturally, she got little sleep while feeding and caring first for one baby and then another. Then, three months later, she became ill with a respiratory condition complicated by a painful sinus infection. Not only was the pain making her miserable, but also it was handicapping her role as a mommy. She tells about that time:

Sinus infections were common in my family. To my dismay, I also began to have them, one after another, leading up to this markedly painful one. The infection was located in the maxillary sinus, on top of the nerves to my teeth on the left side of my mouth. I went to a specialist several times during that ordeal. He drained the sinus cavity twice to relieve the pressure, but most of his efforts to alleviate the pain failed.

He prescribed heavy pain medication, which I was reluctant to take because of nursing two little babies. But because the pain was so excruciating, I had to take the medicine in order to function. However, as the pain became more intense, even a double dose of the prescribed pills gave no relief at all.

One morning I was sitting at the kitchen table, hardly able to cry because of the increasing pain. My husband, Phil, not normally an emotional person, put his hand over the painful area on my face and cried out to God with tears for my healing. Instantly, the pain ended, as if a curtain had fallen over it! It was quite dramatic and took me totally by surprise. My sinuses drained, and I was suddenly well and had increased energy. That miracle happened thirty years ago, and since that time I've not had even one sinus infection.

SURGERY AVOIDED

Recently Mary Beth had another reason to trust God for healing. One day when she was suddenly hit with unbearable abdominal pain, she had to drive herself to the hospital emergency room. Tests revealed that her colon had ruptured and spread dangerous toxins into her abdomen.

Doctors sent her for a CT scan so they could determine the extent of the damage, then for the next five hours tried to remove abscesses from the abdominal cavity. They warned her that she might have to undergo another long session the next day. That night her temperature shot up to 104.8 degrees Fahrenheit. She shook uncontrollably as nurses battled valiantly to bring the fever down to a safe range while IV antibiotics were continually being pumped throughout her body.

The next morning her friend Jackie arrived to pray for her, after having driven for six hours to get to the hospital. At first she knelt to pray. Then she rose to her feet, laid hands on Mary Beth's abdomen, and boldly declared that the spotless Lamb of God was slain for her healing.

"Both of us sensed the tangible presence of the King of kings," Mary Beth said. "I rested peacefully, enjoying every moment of His sweet presence."

An hour later the doctor came to tell her she had to go for another CT scan and that there was a strong possibility she would need a colostomy. He warned her that she might face two surgeries: one to clean out the abdomen and create a colostomy until the intestines were healed, and the second to reattach the colon.

"But the King of kings visited me this morning, and He has healed me," she told him with a smile.

After the tests were run again, she waited with her husband and friend Jackie for the doctor's report. When he finally appeared, along with the doctor who was preparing to do the arduous treatment on her, he looked puzzled.

"I don't know what happened—maybe the antibiotics worked overnight, but it appears that there are no more areas of abscess for us to work on," he said.

"Hallelujah!" Mary Beth shouted.

"She's into the Good Book," her doctor explained to the surgeon.

Jehovah Rophe

> But I will sing of Your power;
> Yes, I will sing aloud of your mercy in the morning;
> For You have been my defense
> And refuge in the day of trouble.
> To You, O my Strength, I will sing praises;
> For God is my defense,
> The God of my mercy.
>
> —PSALM 59:16–17

I am the God who heals thee

Mary Beth continued praising God and singing about Jesus all the way back to her room. The nurses heard her coming and ran to meet her, surprised and glad she was returning so quickly and with such joy.

This story illustrates that God cares about all the hurts in life and that as believers we can ask for our Creator's intervention for ourselves and for others. Her husband, simply out of love and compassion for his wife, cried out to God to touch and heal her. A friend and prayer partner drove many hours to lay hands on Mary Beth and pray for healing. These were ordinary folks crying out to "Daddy God" for help. The Father who is concerned about sinus headaches, abscesses, arthritis, and your baby's nightly colic is also concerned about your healing. Your healing has a higher purpose.

A HIGHER PURPOSE

Jesus, who suffered pain on the cross for us, can readily identify with our pain whether it is short-lived or ongoing. With great compassion for the hurting and the oppressed, He healed people by different means under varying conditions, and He commissioned His followers to do the same.

However, we know that these same people who followed Jesus also suffered in many ways—look at Stephen, Paul, and Silas. Stephen, the first martyr of the church, was stoned to death for his faith in the Lord Jesus. As he was dying, with Saul of Tarsus witnessing the event, he prayed, "Lord, do not hold this sin against them" (Acts 7:60, NIV). Soon after Stephen's martyrdom, Saul had a divine confrontation with Jesus, was converted, and became Paul the Apostle (Acts 9:1–31).

In his own ministry, Paul suffered illness, was beaten, stoned, imprisoned, left for dead, shipwrecked, bitten by a snake, and went days without food (2 Cor. 11:23–28). Yet his epistles are a testament of God's faithfulness in seeing him through every ordeal, and he could declare, "For our light affliction, which is but for a moment, is working for us a far more exceeding and eternal weight of glory" (2 Cor. 4:17).

Silas, Paul's fellow evangelist, was beaten and thrown into prison along with the apostle. Rather than bemoaning their pain and unjust treatment, we read, "But at midnight Paul and Silas were praying and singing hymns to God, and the other prisoners were listening to them" (Acts 16:25). By the end of the chapter the two evangelists were freed, the jailer had been led to Christ, and Paul and Silas continued their missionary journey.

We see a common thread here: the suffering that Jesus and His followers endured was never in vain. It always achieved a higher purpose that brought glory and honor to God. At some point in our lifetime, each of us has suffered the very real bodily discomfort and mental anguish that pain brings. So we know how difficult it is to praise God while feeling overwhelmed by a tidal wave of pain. Yet that is the example we see over and over in Scripture.

Jehovah Rophe

Hear my cry, O God;
Attend to my prayer.
From the end of the earth I will cry to You,
When my heart is overwhelmed;
Lead me to the rock that is higher than I.

For You have been a shelter for me,
And a strong tower from the enemy.

—PSALM 61:1–3

I am the God who heals thee

Bible teacher Joy Dawson suggests that when we or a loved one needs healing, we should "start with worshiping and praising God for *who He is*." Then she proposes that we pray four key prayers:

1. "Dear God, do something in these circumstances that will bring the maximum glory to Your name."

2. "Please tell me what it is You're trying to teach me at this time. Thank You that You will."

3. "In Your way, and in Your time, please reveal to me the purposes and/or causes of this illness. Thank You that You will."

4. "Tell me the next thing that I am to do. Thank You that You will, in Your way and in Your time."[2]

Whether the pain is physical or emotional, we can choose to rely on God's grace to sustain us through the dark days. And we can trust Him to bring us into a deeper level of intimacy with Him

44

as we pass through the trial and become conformed to the image of His Son (Rom. 8:29). Prayer, fasting, anointing with oil, partaking of Holy Communion, meditating on Scripture, and working with medical caregivers are but a few ways people have coped with pain. In some cases, changes in one's way of life and obeying the Holy Spirit's leading can make a huge difference, as Lynda Brooks discovered in her quest for healing. Here is her story in her own words.

———————

About eight years ago I started taking step aerobics at the church I attended. Immediately my feet started hurting badly. I kept on attending class, thinking I would get used to it. But after several months I had to quit. The pain was so severe that medication didn't curb it.

I asked for prayer at church or whenever and wherever I could. But the pain progressed. It became so intense that at one point I wanted to just go on to heaven. I had to either stay in bed or else hobble around like an old lady, so my activities were curtailed drastically.

One day my Sunday school teacher, who had prayed for me for months, called me with hopeful news. She had had a vision of me being healed, in which she saw Jesus and me hugging each other and crying tears of joy. I presumed this meant instant healing—though she hadn't said so. But another year went by before healing came. And it only happened after I chose to make some changes in my attitude and daily habits.

I had become addicted to television. At night when I tossed and turned in agony, I would turn on my TV and watch romance and fantasy shows just to get my mind off the pain. In reality I was allowing garbage into my thought life rather than feeding my spirit on the Word of God. Although I felt the Lord wanted me to give it up, at first I chose not to.

Sometimes, because of the intense pain, I would take more

medication than had been prescribed. Finally, my husband went with me to the doctor. When I told them I was addicted to pain pills and needed help, they determined that from then on, my husband would dole out my medications. I was relieved that the temptation to overdose was taken out of my hands. Then I made some drastic decisions:

- I stopped watching television completely and studied God's Word instead.

- I changed my eating habits by abstaining from sugar and choosing a more healthy diet—this meant I lost weight, which lightened the load on my feet.

- I enrolled in an exercise program at a local gym.

- I allowed the podiatrist to fit me with specially made plastic molds for my shoes (orthotics), which help to balance my weight more evenly and lessen pressure on the ball of my foot.

Within two weeks of my visit to his office I was able to walk without pain. I attribute my healing to the Lord's intervention and my lifestyle changes, along with help from the doctor. In the process I spent more time in prayer and Bible study, and I learned to fine-tune my spiritual ear to hear the Holy Spirit's voice for myself.

I also learned the difference between faith and presumption, as I realized that I couldn't presume I would be healed because of my friend's vision. I had to obey what God was showing me and change my bad habits.

Today I can walk anywhere and am back into the full swing of living, minus medications and TV. I thank God every day for the miracle of being able to walk without pain after eight years of suffering.

⬥⟩⟨⬥

JESUS' OWN PAIN

Jesus always knew He was to be the sacrificial Lamb that would take away the sins of the world. He didn't have to endure the beatings, the nails, and suffering death by crucifixion. He could have called on angels to deliver Him. Yet He chose to endure. For me. For you.

Jehovah Rophe

Although he was a son, he learned obedience from what he suffered and, once made perfect, he became the source of eternal salvation for all who obey him.
—HEBREWS 5:8–9, NIV

I am the God who heals thee

Dr. Paul Brand spent a lifetime as a missionary doctor working with lepers in India and specializing as a hand surgeon. He describes eloquently the significance of Jesus bearing such horrible pain on our behalf:

> Until God took on the soft tissue of flesh…just as subject to abuse as ours, He had not truly experienced pain. By sending His Son to earth, God learned to feel pain the same way we feel pain. Our prayers and cries of suffering take on greater meaning because we now know them to be understood by Him.…He took on Himself the limitations of time and space and family and pain and sorrow.[3]

PAUL'S SUFFERING

Despite the miraculous healings that God performed through the apostle Paul, he wrote of his own struggle with a "thorn in the flesh," which he called "a messenger of Satan" (2 Cor. 12:7–9). Three times he pleaded with the Lord to take it away. But instead of removing it, the Lord said to him, "My grace is sufficient for you, for My strength is made perfect in weakness" (v. 9).

Some scholars, based on Paul's writing in Galatians 4:13–15 and 6:11, believe the "thorn" was a physical ailment, possibly poor eyesight. Others speculate that it could refer to a demonized person who continually harassed him, because Paul spoke of "a messenger of Satan to buffet [or torment] me" (v. 7).

Pastor Jack Hayford provides excellent insight into how each of us can best relate to Paul's experience. He writes:

> God's grace becomes His enablement or empowerment to achieve His plan, endure hardship, or access Him. Paul's struggle has never been defined with certainty, leaving open the possibility of any one of us seeing in God's words to him, words equally applicable to us. His grace is powerful and all-enabling to the believer. His grace facilitates our abilities to conquer every weakness as we yield to an absolute trust or reliance upon God, trusting His heart even when we cannot trace His hand.[4]

Over the past several months while working on this book, I (Ruthanne) have had my own struggle with chronic back and knee pain. One surgeon told me I needed back surgery; another recommended knee replacement. Having no sense of peace about either option, I've been seeking God for His healing as well as for wisdom to change anything I'm doing or not doing to worsen the condition. I'm learning some of the same things Lynda learned—that changing my eating habits and giving more attention to proper nutrition and exercise can improve the situation.

I (Quin) experienced severe neck pain for three years after a head-on crash caused whiplash. Later I fell on an icy street, then endured the agony of trying to walk on a mending broken foot. Pain is sort of the "alarm bell" that goes off to tell us something is troubling our bodies. Yet, over time, our pain diminishes as our bodies heal. Yes, my neck still gets stiff sometimes, and my foot aches in soggy weather. But the severe pain caused by the injuries has dissipated.

DEALING WITH PERSISTENT PAIN

Doctors say the most commonly recurring pain occurs in the back, neck, or joints, although victims of diseases such as cancer may experience pain anywhere. If the pain is persistent, most people try to find the source of it, as did our schoolteacher friend Judy Ball.

Judy's pain simply would not go away. Headaches, dizziness, and pressure in the back of her neck plagued her for six months. When she began to experience slowness when she walked, she knew something was seriously wrong.

Before seeing a doctor about the problem, Judy wanted to be in good spiritual condition, so she and her husband went away to the mountains to fast and pray for three days. "I confessed any sin I felt may be separating me from God's best, and then I asked the Lord to help me order my priorities as I faced this crisis," she told us.

Medical tests revealed a tumor in her brain about the size of a tennis ball, requiring immediate surgery. When she awakened from surgery, she asked the nurse to play her cassette of praise music. As "Behold the Lamb" played quietly, she worshiped the Lord, thanking Him that she could still think, feel, and respond to stimuli.

During the next four days in the hospital, Judy felt the Word of God was literally restoring her as she listened to tapes of Scripture verses on healing. After she went home, she was told to rest—no talking and no visitors.

Jehovah Rophe

> Remember your word to your servant,
>   for you have given me hope.
> My comfort in my suffering is this:
>   Your promise preserves my life....
>
> May your unfailing love be my comfort,
>   according to your promise to your servant.
> —PSALM 119:49–50, 76, NIV

I am the God who heals thee

"I didn't sleep for five days, but I rested in the Lord and meditated on Bible verses," she said. "I regained my strength, but I rearranged my priorities and decided not to go back to work. Eight weeks following surgery I left for a missions trip to Africa, followed by trips to Korea and Israel."

Judy is confident that the days she spent fasting and praying before surgery prepared her spiritually. "During my illness I learned I must always be prepared to meet God. I simply trusted Him—and whether I lived or died, I was in God's hands," she said.

Today she prays for others to be healed and has seen numerous miracles as a result. In the twelve years since her brain tumor surgery, she has served as an intercessor for several large ministries and has gone on prayer journeys to many nations, including fifteen trips to Israel.[5]

SHE SURVIVED A DEADLY ACCIDENT AND CANCER

My (Quin's) friend Hilda was just forty when she had a boating accident that almost took her life. She survived and underwent twenty-two major surgeries to put her crushed face back together. In the process of her recovery, she and her husband were baptized in the Holy Spirit and became active in full gospel meetings.

But five years after her boating ordeal, a cancer surgeon discovered a malignant melanoma. He removed most of the upper arm muscle and all the glands under her left arm, then grafted skin from her leg onto the affected area.

"Possibly only three months to live," she overheard the doctor tell her husband as she awakened from surgery. *Is this a death sentence?* she wondered.

"I returned home in excruciating pain, as the skin graft did not heal and boils developed all around it," she remembers. "After God had seen me through all my surgeries following the boating accident, I had taught on faith and healing in many churches in Alabama. But now I was facing the loneliest time of my life."

Jehovah Rophe

> News about him spread all over Syria, and people brought to him all who were ill with various diseases, those suffering severe pain, the demon-possessed, those having seizures, and the paralyzed, and he healed them.
> —MATTHEW 4:24, NIV

I am the God who heals thee

One day in prayer Hilda simply said, "Father, until now I have not asked why the boat propeller sliced my face. But now I am going to ask you why about this cancer."

Immediately Hilda sensed that God's presence filled the room. She felt as if Jesus sat on her bed and said, "Until now you have learned what I can do for you. Now I want you to know Me." As she lay there weeping, she suddenly thought of a verse: "Though he slay me, yet will I trust in him" (Job 13:15, KJV).

"I repeated those words, and the minute they came out of my mouth, the pain left," she said. "From then on I began to heal. I was on a new path of not only trusting God, but also of seeking Him with all my heart." Hilda pored over Bible passages for hours, learning a new dimension of prayer as she spent more time with the Lord in her quiet time.

Today Hilda has passed the seventy-year mark and has even out-lived her husband, but she still seeks God with all her heart! She knows that while doctors did all they could, it was Jesus who did the real healing in her body and heart. I talk with her frequently by phone and am astounded by her energy and enthusiasm.

"The Lord is my best friend and husband now," she told me recently. "I pray with two groups at my church each week, but my greatest ministry is to my grandchildren."[6]

QUIN'S MOM'S BOUT WITH PAIN

It seems like yesterday—though it was twenty years ago—that Easter afternoon as my mom struggled with the final stages of cancer. "Why is she suffering so?" one of my children asked at her bedside.

"I don't know," I replied. "I've asked that question a hundred times myself. All I know is, if we suffer with Christ we will reign with him." (See 2 Timothy 2:12, KJV.) Then I unfolded a letter Mom had written to her children three months earlier and gave it to her to read:

> ...I've needed God's grace to see me through. One of the hard things about suffering is that when others learn you are suf-fering, they get involved and suffer, too. I know Jesus' pur-pose in suffering on the cross was to bring us to God. He suffered for us. The other night I said, "Lord, give me grace

to endure. I want this to be an opportunity, not an ordeal. I don't want to have any bad feelings." It was as if the big floodgates instantly opened. The grace and love of God flooded my being. Everything changed in me.... Since then I've felt the joy of the Lord and His grace, and know that peace which passes all understanding will sustain and carry me through. I trust this will be an opportunity and not an ordeal for each of you, too. I want you to know God's grace is sufficient for you. My future is in God's hands, and whatever the need, it will be met when that time arrives.

All my love, Mother.

Though she was suffering and unable to talk to us, I knew Mom had settled the issue about her suffering days earlier when she experienced God's floodgates. He had filled her with love, peace, and assurance of a future home with no suffering.

What a comfort to know that even in times of pain and suffering, we can press in to "know Christ and the power of his resurrection and the fellowship of sharing in his sufferings..." (Phil. 3:10, NIV).

Dr. Brand ends his book by asking the thought-provoking question: "Why did Christ keep His scars?" Then he writes:

He could have had a perfect body, or no body, when He returned to splendor in heaven. Instead He carried with Him remembrances of His visit to earth. For a reminder of His time here, He chose scars. That is why I say God hears and understands our pain, and even absorbs it into Himself— because He kept those scars as a lasting image of wounded humanity. He has been here; He has borne the sentence. The pain of man has become the pain of God.[7]

Yes, He still cares about your pain and suffering. And in the midst of it all, He wants to give you peace. Our next chapter will explore ways that you can achieve this peace that comes only from Him.

PRAYER

Jesus, I worship and praise You, thankful that because You suffered on the cross for me, You can identify with what I feel. Lord, sometimes I hurt so badly I don't think I can take much more. Please help me through this. Give me strength to endure. When You walked on the earth You reached out to heal those suffering with severe pain. Lord, I need that healing touch from You right now. Thank You that I can always call out to You in my pain. I praise You right now for Your presence and Your comfort. Amen.

I understand the buffeted days and the days of no small tempest, when neither sun nor stars appear. And it is good to pass through such days, for if we didn't we could neither prove our God nor help others. If any experience of ours helps to bring others to our Lord, what does any buffeting matter?

But we are not meant to live in a perpetual stormy sea. We are meant to pass through and find harbor and so be at peace. Then we are free from occupation with ourselves and our storms—free to help others.

I want to live in the light of the thought of His coming, His triumph—the end of this present darkness, the glory of His seen Presence. This bathes the present in radiance.[1]

—*Amy Carmichael*

4

Lord,

I NEED PEACE

Peace I leave with you, My peace I give to you; not as the world gives do I give to you. Let not your heart be troubled, neither let it be afraid.

—JOHN 14:27

ARE YOU FACING a frightening surgery or the diagnosis of a dreaded disease? Do rumors of a worldwide flu epidemic or the discovery of new diseases strike fear to your heart?

When you suffer a disabling injury or learn you have a serious illness, it may seem as if you've been hit by a violent storm. Perhaps you feel powerless as waves of anxiety and hopelessness engulf you. But that is just the time when Jesus can give you His peace.

The disciples once were at sea when a sudden storm hit, and they were inundated by waves that threatened to sink the boat. Though Jesus was with them in the boat, He was asleep and seemingly oblivious to their distress. Maybe you, like the disciples, are wondering, *Doesn't Jesus even care about this crisis I'm facing?* But when they called on Him, He immediately spoke to the wind and the sea, and they became calm (Matt. 8:26).

These things I have spoken to you, that in Me you may have peace. In the world you will have tribulation; but be of good cheer, I have overcome the world.

—JOHN 16:33

Even in the midst of your storm of doubts, questions, and fears about your health crisis, Jesus can quiet the tumult and sustain you with His peace.

CHOOSING TO ABIDE IN PEACE

Dick and Sharon Spencer found this to be true when they learned that at age sixty-nine, Dick was in the advanced stages of congestive heart failure, and his kidneys were on the verge of shutting down. Almost eleven years earlier this pastor in Midland, Texas, had undergone a quintuple bypass and came through the ordeal to a prolonged season of improved health.

Now doctors said not only were his kidneys failing, but also that his heart would not last much longer. Unless they could find a way to reverse the kidney failure, one doctor estimated he could have only two days to live.

Dick's son, Greg, called the congregation together for a healing prayer service in which they prayed over a pillowcase and anointed it with oil. Greg and Sharon also called several out-of-town friends, including me (Ruthanne), asking us to pray. The hometown cardiologist referred him to a specialist in Austin, and they flew Dick there for an evaluation. Sharon made sure the anointed pillowcase was with him for the journey. After a series of tests, the Austin doctors determined that they could not help him, so he returned home and within twenty-four hours was back in the hospital again.

"The situation looked really grim by this time—the doctors wanted to refer me to hospice care," Dick remembers. "But I had absolutely no fear. Despite the negative reports the doctors gave me, I really believed that God would heal me one way or another."

Jehovah Rophe

> Be anxious for nothing, but in everything by prayer and supplication, with thanksgiving, let your requests be made known to God; and the peace of God, which surpasses all understanding, will guard your hearts and minds through Christ Jesus. Finally...whatever things are just, whatever things are pure, whatever things are lovely, whatever things are of good report, if there is any virtue and if there is anything praiseworthy—meditate on these things.
>
> —PHILIPPIANS 4:6–8

I am the God who heals thee

Through connections with former classmates, a doctor at the Texas Heart Institute in Houston agreed to review his case. After going over all Dick's records, he said if his hometown doctors could get his kidneys functioning at an acceptable level, they would accept him and consider him for a heart transplant. A major prayer alert went out, and within two days, he was flown to Houston.

"While I was lying on a stretcher on the plane, I felt God spoke four things to me very clearly," Dick reported. "First, He said, 'Be strong and courageous,' which I didn't understand at the time. Then He said, 'My hand is upon you…I will surround you with My people…your miracle is at hand.' I shared with my wife what the Lord had told me and declared those words with complete confidence that I would come through this experience."

They took Dick to CCU where a specialist examined him, looked at his dossier, and said, "You'll be spending some time here." As it turned out, he was away from home for twenty weeks, most of them in that Houston hospital.

The buildup of fluids in his body was so severe that it took two weeks for doctors to get the fluid levels under control. As they also struggled to get his lung pressure down to an acceptable level, a committee of doctors reviewed Dick's case almost daily and considered various options for treatment. At the same time he had to undergo many other additional tests to be sure all his other organs were functioning normally before he would be approved as a heart transplant candidate.

One day a research physician "just happened" to drop in on this committee meeting and asked what the problem was. After they explained all the complications in Dick's case, the research specialist suggested they try inserting a balloon pump into his heart—an idea they hadn't even considered. They immediately rushed Dick to surgery.

Two days later one of the leading surgeons at the hospital came into his room, checked the monitors he was hooked up to, and said, "It appears you've had providential intervention. Your lung pressure is reduced enough to put you on the list of candidates to receive a new heart."

This was great news, but the next few weeks would bring the greatest challenge Dick had ever faced. He had to remain flat on his back with his legs completely stationary while the balloon pump took over the work of pumping blood through his body.

A New Heart

Now the search was on to find a heart that was a match for Dick's size, blood type, and so on. After two weeks of keeping him stationary on a special mattress to prevent bedsores, doctors told Dick and his family that a nineteen-year-old patient in critical condition in a nearby hospital was not expected to live. The young man's family had signed all the papers necessary to donate his heart when he expired.

"We have to pray for him to be healed," Dick said when he got this report. He had prayed for the sick for years and had seen hundreds of people healed through prayer, so this was just a normal response for him. After asking those in the room to agree with him, Dick prayed that the young man's life would be spared. Sure enough, his condition reversed and he recovered, so that heart was not available after all.

But within twenty-four hours another heart that was a perfect match—this one from a twenty-year-old man—became available and was being flown to Houston from out of state. Doctors immediately prepped Dick for surgery, and the five-hour transplant operation began as soon as the new heart arrived.

After surgery there were continuing problems with Dick's lungs, resulting in many painful procedures and tests. "While I was enduring all this misery and more pain than I had ever experienced, I kept remembering God's word to me," Dick said. "Now I understood why He said, 'Be strong and courageous.'

"During this time my wife was my greatest encourager, even on the days when I felt grumpy. She stayed in a hotel near the hospital and came into my room every morning with a new verse of Scripture and words of faith that helped us stay focused on God's promises."

Sharon rallied a whole network of intercessors to pray for Dick. As events transpired she would pass on reports to one of these intercessors, who periodically sent out e-mail updates, along with scriptures to pray.

"When they insert the new heart into the body and attach it to the arteries, that heart has been on ice for four to six hours," Dick explained. "But as soon as they release clamps on the two main arteries, allowing blood to flow into it, the heart immediately begins to beat. Doctors are amazed by this phenomenon, but it is actually stated in Leviticus 17:11, 'For the life of the flesh is in the blood.'"

One day after surgery, when his condition was stable and he was on the long road to full recovery, a doctor from Israel who had worked on Dick's case came by his room. "Doctor, I know I was in bad shape when I arrived here," Dick said to him, "but just how bad was I?"

"The average person's heart functions at a 45 to 50 percent capacity," the doctor replied. "By the time you got here, your heart was down to only 2 to 3 percent output. You couldn't have lasted much longer. However, you had a stronger will to live than the average patient has."

After many weeks in the hospital, Dick went to outpatient status, and he and Sharon stayed in a small apartment near the hospital. He had to be checked regularly to see that his lungs were functioning properly and to be sure his body was not rejecting the new heart. Every time a problem arose, a new prayer bulletin went out. This was the time when they stood on the words God had spoken to him on the airplane and on two scriptures they had claimed from the beginning:

> You shall also decide and decree a thing, and it shall be established for you; and the light [of God's favor] shall shine upon your ways.
>
> —Job 22:28, amp

> I shall not die but live, and shall declare the works and recount the illustrious acts of the Lord.
>
> —Psalm 118:17, amp

FAR-REACHING RESULTS

During all those weeks in the hospital, Dick shared his faith with doctors, nurses, technicians, custodians—almost everyone with whom he had any contact while he was conscious. He has counted more than sixty people, representing more than twelve countries—including a Muslim limo driver—who have accepted Christ and received a Bible from him. A missionary friend in Houston supplied him with Bibles whenever he needed them.

"Every time we go back to the hospital for another checkup, another person accepts the Lord," he reported. "Recently a heart surgeon asked me to autograph his Bible and write a word of encouragement to him. My main cardiologist told me that one of his most precious possessions is his new Bible, which he now reads to his six-year-old son every night before he goes to sleep. I told him that God allowed me to get a new physical heart so that all these medical people could get new spiritual hearts."

Dick has now passed his two-year checkup with flying colors. His organ rejection level is zero, his fluid levels are normal, and he says he feels better than he's felt for twenty years. He lifts weights and does two miles on the treadmill every day—one mile uphill. He spends eight hours in the office five days a week and preaches three times every week. He and Sharon look forward to the time they'll be able to make their first missions trip since his surgery. He believes God supplied him with a new heart simply because his ministry on this earth is not yet finished.

Pastor Dick and Sharon passed through a storm fiercer than they could have imagined. But through it all they experienced God's peace and in the end received the miracle that He had promised. The people who received Christ and the critically ill nineteen-year-old who recovered after prayer were part of the overflow.

Several factors were at work in this amazing story:

- Prayers of agreement by the congregation and other prayer partners
- Anointed pillowcase that was prayed over
- God's promises given to Dick on the airplane
- Several Scripture verses they were declaring
- His wife's unwavering faith and encouragement
- Continuous prayer coverage by a network of intercessors who received e-mail updates with prayer points and scriptures
- Expert care by a team of specialists and surgeons
- Miraculous provision of a heart that was compatible for him to receive
- Dick's willingness to comply with doctors' orders regarding exercise and diet, which was critical to his successful recovery

"Our pastor has a new heart—a really new heart!" the e-mail praise report read. I (Ruthanne) will never forget the day I got that message, after weeks of praying with the many intercessors who stood with Dick and Sharon through those critical weeks.

GUIDELINES FOR PRAYER

Obviously, prayer played a vital role in Pastor Dick's miracle. These days, people in the medical field are more interested than ever before in exploring the effect that prayer has on people dealing with critical illness. In 2004, a survey of 31,000 adults released by the U.S. Centers for Disease Control and Prevention found that 43 percent of U.S. adults prayed for their own health, and 24 percent asked others to pray for them.[2]

A lot of people, whether they're Christians or not, turn to prayer when they face a health dilemma. Sadly, many of these actually know very little of what the Bible teaches on this important subject. Let's examine some of the prayer methods that we and other intercessors have found to be effective.

At the top of our list is the prayer of agreement—which means praying with a spouse and/or one or more prayer partners. To begin, we suggest you ask the Lord to show you how He wants you to pray, thus assuring that you are praying in agreement with the Holy Spirit.

Jehovah Rophe

> Likewise the Spirit also helps in our weaknesses. For we do not know what we should pray for as we ought, but the Spirit Himself makes intercession for us with groanings which cannot be uttered. Now He who searches the hearts knows what the mind of the Spirit is, because He makes intercession for the saints according to the will of God.
>
> —ROMANS 8:26–27

I am the God who heals thee

Jesus said, "If two of you agree on earth concerning anything that they ask, it will be done for them by My Father in heaven. For where two or three are gathered together in My name, I am there in the midst of them" (Matt. 18:19–20). The word *agree* in this scripture is from a Greek root from which we get our English word "symphony." It means "to be in harmony or accord concerning a matter."[3]

Fasting, particularly when done in agreement with one or more other intercessors, is effective in praying for healing, as well as for other situations. After Dick returned home following his heart transplant, Sharon established the habit of fasting every Monday as she prayed for Dick's complete recovery. Her daughter-in-law, Angela, became one of her close prayer partners and often joined her in fasting.

Prayer points to consider as you pray for healing:

- Pray for God's guidance in seeking the best solution to the health problem. This could include vitamin therapy, diet changes, physical therapy, an exercise program, and/or choosing the best physician available for the ailment.

- Pray preventive prayers. For example: that all medical personnel will be alert and do their very best work in treating the illness; that there will be no mistakes, wrong judgments, or wrong decisions made by any of these people in prescribing medication or treatment.

- Pray that medications will be beneficial, with no harmful reactions or side effects.

- Pray that no infections develop following surgery or hospital treatment, and that high standards of hygiene be observed.

- Pray against all negative words written or spoken by medical professionals, friends, family members, or anyone else. Their word is not final; God's Word is!

- Pray in the Spirit—this can mean praying in your prayer language, which assures you are praying according to the will of God. (See Romans 8:26–27.) Or it can mean being specifically led by the Holy Spirit as you "pray with your mind." (See 1 Corinthians 14:15.)

- Proclaim the Word of God and His promises over the situation—this helps reinforce your own faith as well as that of others involved. You can also paraphrase verses into Scripture prayers, inserting the name of the person you're praying for.

- Walk in a spirit of praise and thanksgiving, playing praise music and singing Scripture songs. This, along with declaring Scripture, strengthens you against fear.

- Fast as you are led by the Holy Spirit. Spend some of your fasting time in prayer, worship, and Scripture reading.

- Make sure you are not harboring any unforgiveness against anyone so as not to give place to the devil. (See 2 Corinthians 2:10–11; Ephesians 4:26–27.)

- Partake of the Lord's Supper as often as you are led, remembering the death and resurrection of Jesus Christ and what He accomplished on the cross for man's spirit, soul, and body. (See Isaiah 53:4–6.)

A SACRAMENTAL HEALING

For Peggy Davis, taking Holy Communion became the "medicine of life," a term used by a fourth-century bishop in referring to the Eucharist.[4]

One evening as she stood by the back door of her car at dusk, she saw the headlights of a black beach buggy barreling right toward her. The vehicle hit her, propelling her onto the top of the car hood, where her head banged against the windshield. She went flying through the air before landing on the asphalt road.

Lord, do something. I can't stand this pain, she prayed silently as intense pain in her leg became almost unbearable. When her husband and sister reached her, they thought she was dead. She heard someone say her left leg was bleeding a lot, and then a woman nearby started praying for her recovery.

In the ambulance she and her husband recited the Lord's Prayer together. Once she got to the hospital it took more than a hundred stitches to close the gap in her left leg; the artery had been severed in two places. While the doctor stitched, her pastor held her hand and prayed for her. A group from her church huddled in another part of the hospital praying. Medical tests indicated that she had a skull fracture and internal bleeding, and her doctor told her he intended to operate the next day.

The following morning her pastor returned to give her Holy Communion before she was to go to surgery. As he did, she heard the familiar prayer she repeated each Sunday, beseeching our merciful Father "to grant that, by the merits and death of Thy Son Jesus Christ, and through faith in His blood, we, and all Thy whole church, may obtain remission of our sins, and all other benefits of His passion." Peggy shares in her own words what transpired:

———◆◈◆———

I cannot explain what happened next, but something mystical and supernatural occurred as I took the bread. The pastor continued reading from the *Book of Common Prayer*: "The body of our Lord Jesus Christ, which was given for thee, preserve thy body and soul unto everlasting life. Take and eat this in remembrance that Christ died for thee and feed on Him in thy heart by faith, and with thanksgiving."

As I swallowed the wine, he continued reading, "The blood of our Lord Jesus Christ, which was shed for thee, preserve thy body and soul into everlasting life. Drink this in remembrance that Christ's blood was shed for thee and be thankful."

While I was in that hospital bed, my Lord reached down and touched me. The power of His Holy Spirit wrapped around me, and I knew I was healed.

The doctor came in, reevaluated my tests, and ordered new X-rays. I wasn't surprised when he later walked into my room with good news. "I came to the hospital this morning prepared to operate on you," he said. "But now we won't have to—the internal bleeding has stopped."

———————————◆✦◆✦◆———————————

Peggy believes that when she received the elements of Holy Communion, the healing took place. Even the skull fracture failed to show up on the new X-rays. She went home after only five days in the hospital. The next Sunday she walked down the aisle of the church on crutches to receive Holy Communion at the altar rail. Tears spilled down her face as she praised God for her healing.

It has been more than thirty years since Peggy's accident. But she has told her story many times, emphasizing that as she took Communion in the hospital she experienced a totally new understanding of Christ's body being broken for her, His blood being shed for her sins, and His stripes taken for her healing.[5]

Jehovah Rophe

Grace to you and peace from God our Father and the Lord Jesus Christ. We give thanks to the God and Father of our Lord Jesus Christ, praying always for you, since we heard of your faith in Christ Jesus and of your love for all the saints; because of the hope which is laid up for you in heaven....

—COLOSSIANS 1:2–5

I am the God who heals thee

"I feel the Lord's presence so close to me whenever I take the sacrament of Holy Communion," Peggy told me (Quin) recently. "It gives me strength for the day and for whatever I will face in the week ahead. I have felt God's touch so many times while kneeling at the altar rail to receive the elements. I like to take Communion as often as possible," she added.

Who can understand how a person can be healed during the Eucharist—meaning "giving of thanks"? This sacrament, along with water baptism, has been practiced by Christians since the days of the New Testament up to the present time. Before serving Holy Communion, many groups often read this familiar passage:

> For I received from the Lord that which I also delivered to you: that the Lord Jesus on the same night in which He was betrayed took bread; and when He had given thanks, He broke it and said, "Take, eat; this is My body which is broken for you; do this in remembrance of Me." In the same manner He also took the cup after supper, saying, "This cup is the new covenant in My blood. This do, as often as you drink it, in remembrance of Me." For as often as you eat this bread and drink this cup, you proclaim the Lord's death till He comes.
> —1 Corinthians 11:23–26

In the church I (Ruthanne) grew up in, our small congregation observed the Lord's Supper once a month as everyone knelt at the altar or at the front row of seats. I remember one Sunday when our pastor taught on the truth that Jesus provided healing for us in the Atonement, according to Isaiah 53:5 and 1 Peter 2:24. He encouraged those who had physical needs to trust God to heal them as they partook of the bread.

A man in the church—a new believer, as I recall, whose broken leg was in a cast—went to the altar on crutches and managed to kneel. God's presence was very real during our time of worship and taking Communion that morning. Suddenly, the man began rejoicing with his arms upraised, shouting, "I'm healed! I'm healed!" After the service he took out his pocket knife, cut the cast off his leg, and walked out of the building carrying his crutches.

Many have received healing while taking the Lord's Supper. When our friend Chuck Pierce was invited to minister in Nigeria, he hesitated to accept because of an infirmity he had struggled with for some time. But in the end he agreed to go and trust God for his physical need. One night, during a prayer meeting attended by ten thousand people, the Spirit of God came. When Communion was about to be served, leaders invited the sick to come forward. Chuck was first in line.

"I felt a curse of infirmity leave my body when I participated," he reported. "I cannot say that I have never been sick again, but what has happened is that a power to resist sickness is now resident. When the power of infirmity comes against me, I submit to God, resist the devil and watch him flee."[6]

But a prayer of agreement also can lead to someone's healing. Our next story shows how God honored the obedience of an older woman who prayed in agreement for a younger woman she was mentoring—even though she didn't feel very spiritually awake or alert when the call came.

An Overnight Miracle

Lori Powers, mom of three and a church secretary, didn't always believe in miracles, but she certainly does now. "The idea that I could personally experience a miracle was just new to me," she said.

One winter evening she put a liquid-sealed freezable plastic bowl containing sweet potatoes in her microwave to warm it up. She thinks she probably left it in too long. When she lifted the bowl out of the microwave with her left hand, it suddenly exploded. As searing pain shot through her hand like hot flames, she screamed so loud it scared her children. Running to the sink, she doused her hand with cold water, then she fainted.

When she came to, she drove herself to the emergency room, hanging her left hand out the window so the cold sleet falling could cool it. As soon as she arrived at the emergency room, a nurse was assigned to go into the treatment area with her for fear she might pass out again.

The doctor told her she had second-degree burns and that her hand would be severely scarred. He applied medication, then bandaged her hand and told her to change the bandage the next day.

As soon as she got home, Lori called Julia, her "spiritual mom," and asked her to pray. Julia had already gone to bed and didn't feel so "spiritual" when the phone rang late that night. But she immediately responded by praying that God would take away Lori's pain, make her hand whole, and give her and her children peace.

Jehovah Rophe

The LORD sits as King forever.
The LORD will give strength to His people;
The LORD will bless His people with peace.
—PSALM 29:10–11

I am the God who heals thee

As Julia prayed, peace descended over Lori, and the pain lessened. Though Julia hadn't felt particularly spiritual at the time, Lori sensed God's anointing as she came into agreement with her friend's prayer for healing. That night her children and husband also prayed for her, and she finally fell asleep.

The next day when she went to work at the church, her pastor inquired about her bandaged hand. Lori told him about the accident, mentioning that the doctor had said she'd probably have scars. Later that same day she removed the bandage to change it, but what she saw amazed her and everyone else who would later see it. Her burned hand was healed—no scars, just one tiny little blister. The rest was much like a newborn baby's skin. She felt that little blister was an indicator of what her whole hand would have looked like without God's healing touch.

That evening when she went to the city's Christmas parade, she saw the nurse who had accompanied her to the hospital treatment room. When Lori showed her the miracle hand, the nurse said, "That is not the hand you burned—let me see the other one. Yes, it is the hand. That makes me believe that God is real!"

Lori said it was worth all the pain if it helped someone believe in God. Certainly it strengthened her own faith and that of others as her pastor invited her to share her story before their congregation.

Even though Julia hadn't felt up to par to pray that night, God worked through her prayers to heal her young friend. We don't have to feel holy, nor do we have to be able to use what may be considered the "right words" to say. We need only to be obedient and in tune with how God wants us to pray.

Another aspect of obedience is to try to understand our situation from God's perspective and respond accordingly. We'll look into this topic in the following chapter.

PRAYER

Lord Jesus, I thank You that You are with me in this storm of uncertainty over my health. Come, calm the tempest and give me Your peace. Guide me through these troubled waters and keep my heart from being afraid. Lord, I put my trust in You for my healing. Thank You for Your presence and for Your promise that You will never forsake me. Amen.

When your eyes are upon your symptoms and your mind is occupied with them more than with God's Word, you have in the ground…seeds of doubt. You are trying to raise one kind of crop from another kind of seed. It is impossible to sow tares and reap wheat. Your symptoms may point you to death, but God's Word points you to life, and you cannot look in these opposite directions at the same time.[1]

—*F. F. Bosworth*

5

Lord,

I NEED PERSPECTIVE

By faith in the name of Jesus, this man whom you see and
know was made strong. It is Jesus' name and the faith that
comes through him that has given this complete healing to
him, as you can all see.

—PETER'S SERMON IN ACTS 3:16, NIV

GETTING GOD'S PERSPECTIVE on the matter when we are in
the midst of a health crisis is not easy. We tend to just want a quick
deliverance from the stress, pain, and worry the problem brings.
"Lord, please help me to get through this" is a sincere cry, a heart-
felt prayer.

But let's not forget that God's concept of time is different from
ours. In His perspective, the process may be every bit as important as the end goal. Ultimately, as we pray we must be honest with
God and with ourselves to determine if there's something at the
root of our illness that we need to address.

For example, do we need to purify our motives? Is there something blocking our relationship with Him? Is there perhaps a

bondage we need to acknowledge, then get rid of? Is there pent-up anger, frustration, unforgiveness, or bitterness toward someone who has wronged us? We may need to spend time in prayer regarding these issues, then write down His responses. Maybe unbelief is the hindering factor in our faith walk. It's important that we truthfully tell God how we feel.

HEART-CHANGE CAN BRING HEALTH-CHANGE

When our car gets sluggish, we ask a mechanic to test it to determine the problem. Similarly, when we become physically ill, we usually go to the doctor for a diagnosis and medical advice. But just as the sluggish car may need an engine overhaul to get it in tune, we may discover that we need a heart-change before we get a health-change.

Jesus commands us to forgive as a condition to our receiving His forgiveness. He tells the story in Matthew 18 of the unmerciful servant who had been forgiven much debt, yet refused to forgive a fellow servant what he owed him.

The master calls the man before him and says, "You wicked servant! I forgave you all that debt because you begged me. Should you not also have had compassion on your fellow servant, just as I had pity on you?" (vv. 32–33).

In anger, the master turns him over to the jailers to be tortured, and Jesus says, "So My heavenly Father also will do to you if each of you, from his heart, does not forgive his brother his trespasses" (v. 35). The sad truth is that in some cases, various forms of sickness may be the "torture" that results from an unwillingness to forgive.

Once after I (Ruthanne) had finished teaching for a home Bible

There is something deeper than happiness, and that is joy. Happiness comes from happenings, but joy may be within in spite of happenings. "Happiness" is the world's word; "joy" is the Christian's word. The New Testament does not use the word "happiness" or promise it—it uses the word "joy." And for a reason.

When the Christian doesn't find joy on account of his happenings, he can always find joy in spite of them.[1]

—*E. Stanley Jones*

7

Lord,
RESTORE MY JOY

The Spirit of the Lord GOD is upon Me,
Because the LORD has anointed Me...
To comfort all who mourn,
To console those who mourn in Zion,
To give them beauty for ashes,
The oil of joy for mourning,
The garment of praise for the spirit of heaviness.

—ISAIAH 61:1–3

OY IN THE midst of this pain? Are you kidding? Admittedly, most of us might find it hard to experience anything even close to joy when we are struggling with pain. But thankfully, God sent the gift of the Holy Spirit to give us joy, hope, and comfort. The Holy Spirit was also sent to reveal spiritual truth, to help us to pray, and to edify our spirits.

To appropriate this gift we need to invite the Holy Spirit to guide us through each day moment by moment, helping us to stay centered on God's promise and provision. This Helper, the gift of the Father to us, will walk with us through our various stages and seasons. Even when we don't know how to pray, the Holy Spirit can pray through us according to God's will (Rom. 8:26–27).

THE JOY OF THE LORD BRINGS LAUGHTER

How can a family that has experienced three bouts with cancer still find joy? Gloria Butler will tell you it's because of their steadfast trust in God, their relationship with the Holy Spirit, and because they believe in laughing a lot, even during hard times.

Gloria knows a lot about hard times—not only is she a survivor of cancer, but so are her husband and her son. Yet the joy of the Lord is her strength, and that coupled with prayer and humor has helped this family through each crisis.

In 1995, when her twenty-four-year-old son, John, was diagnosed with testicular cancer, Gloria's family and prayer partners rallied to pray for his recovery. He had surgery to remove his right testicle, then three weeks later doctors did a lymph node dissection. It was a huge answer to prayer that they found no malignancy in his lymph nodes, so he didn't have to go through chemotherapy. His greatest joy came three months later at the birth of his baby daughter, Cecily. He's now been cancer free for more than ten years.

Gloria told me (Quin) that after she heard me speak in Florida some years ago, she bought our book *A Woman's Guide to Spiritual Warfare*, which she found especially helpful while praying for her son to be restored to health.

"I would close the doors and tell everyone I needed to be alone," she said. "Then I would march around the living room reading the scriptures from your book on spiritual warfare and praying loudly.

I got specific prayers and strategy that helped me through some tough situations."

Two years later, Gloria's husband, John Sr., had lymphoma cancer in his groin, which required surgery, followed by radiation and chemotherapy. When he had his head shaved, family members enjoyed teasing him, jokingly calling him "Mr. Clean" or "Kojak."

Jehovah Rophe

He [God] will yet fill your mouth with laughing, and your lips with rejoicing.

—Job 8:21

I am the God who heals thee

"We found that laughing about anything we could find helped us through—and we laughed a lot," Gloria said. "As Christians we believe we are in a win-win situation. We live for the Lord and receive His blessings, and if we die, we will be with the Lord. So either way we are victors. We have overcome a lot in our lives— my husband has been cancer free for over eight years. We couldn't do it without the joy of the Lord."

One of John's favorite sayings is, "Since the world didn't give me this joy, it can't take it away."

When Gloria went in for a checkup in August 2001, doctors ran tests that showed a growth on her thyroid gland. A few months later they did a biopsy, and the report said it was benign. But during the summer of 2002 she felt increasingly tired and listless and had a cold she couldn't get rid of, so she insisted on having her thyroid removed. The doctor agreed to operate, and to his surprise, it was malignant.

The surgery left her with vocal cord paralysis. Barely able to make a sound, she was forced to communicate mainly by whispering and writing notes. By November it was no better.

One evening her seven-year-old granddaughter, Cecily, laid her hands on her throat and prayed a simple prayer: "Lord, heal Grandma's vocal cords."

"I woke up the next morning and could speak clearly," Gloria said. "The doctor says I still have vocal cord paralysis, but that my right one just 'overcompensates' for the other. I had two radioactive iodine treatments, and I still take medication because I have no thyroid. But I've been talking ever since Cecily prayed for me, and that was over three years ago!"

This family has long believed in the power of God to heal, although they are also thankful for what medical science can do to treat cancer. But they're especially grateful for the intercessors who have stood in the prayer gap with them through each trauma.

Gloria and her friend Irene have been prayer partners for eighteen years. Once each year they go to a campground for a week of prayer, fellowship, and fun together. She also meets weekly with a group of praying women. "Getting through our cancer episodes was so much easier with prayer support," she said. "It helped keep our focus on the Lord and the joy only He can give."

CHOOSING JOY

Scripture tells us, "A cheerful heart is good medicine, but a crushed spirit dries up the bones" (Prov. 17:22, NIV). But now and then we have to decide to choose joy even when our circumstances may appear really grim. Here are some ways of doing this:

- Recall something worthwhile that you can praise God for today—a gorgeous sunset, a rainbow, a phone call, a letter, someone's smile. Count your blessings, reviewing them aloud or writing them in a journal.

- Let go of worry—it saps your energy. Find Bible verses that deal with "be not anxious" and memorize some of them.

- Talk to a positive friend today via phone or e-mail, and try to keep positive people around you. Don't beat up on yourself if you have "down" days, but determine not to stay in a depressed mode.

- Make wise choices about how you spend your leisure time, what you eat, what you watch or listen to, how you exercise, and those with whom you "hang out."

- Find something silly to laugh about, even if you have to dig into your memory bank and pull up a hilarious incident from the past or remember a funny joke.

Our friend Pastor Dutch Sheets provides good advice for moving from despair to joy:

> We must draw near to the Lord in order to see Him there at the point of our pain. It is in His presence that healing comes and we experience fullness of joy (Ps. 16:11).
>
> One of the ways we draw near is through praise and worship. I know it sounds terribly simplistic—and I would never make light of your pain—but I believe that any person's life could be radically and forever changed by extreme doses of praise and worship. Simply applying worship in the same way that one would therapy ... would create a place for the Lord to set up His throne in our hearts (see Psalm 22:3).[2]

Our next story illustrates the power of having supportive people around you who encourage you to walk in the Lord's joy and press through to victory.

THE JOY OF THE LORD IS YOUR STRENGTH

Gaby Crow, twenty-nine, is my (Ruthanne's) Mexican friend who has been my interpreter for some of my ministry trips to Mexico. In mid-2003, when she developed problems with bleeding from the colon, she immediately consulted a doctor. Four months later there was no improvement though she'd followed his advice, so she went to another doctor, who did a special colon scan and a biopsy. The results were devastating: a rapidly growing tumor in an advanced stage of cancer.

"We have to take it out as soon as possible," the doctor said when he gave Gaby the report.

"I know God is with me," she told him. "Let's do whatever it takes to get rid of the problem." Her husband, Jeremy, an American missionary who grew up in Mexico, supported her decision.

Five days later two surgeons performed the operation, but after removing the diseased section of the colon, they encountered problems trying to sew the intestinal tract back together. After five or six hours, a surgeon came out and reported to Jeremy that because of the damage to Gaby's colon, they had to install a colostomy. He mentioned the difficulty they had in getting everything stitched back together properly, but said another surgeon "just happened" to come on the scene and finished up the job nicely.

Neither Gaby nor any of her family members at the hospital that day ever saw this third surgeon, and no one on the staff seemed to know his name. She and Jeremy choose to believe that God sent an angel to help the doctors out!

Her recovery went fairly quickly, and soon she was eating normally and managing her life with the colostomy, which she always believed would be temporary. Although they felt they had gotten all the cancer, doctors wanted her to have radiation and chemotherapy as a precaution.

"I prayed and felt I needed to do what I could about the problem, then trust God to do what only He could do," Gaby said.

Her first stage of treatment was a combination of radiation and chemotherapy sessions spaced out over an eight-month period, and everything seemed to go smoothly. "After several sessions, my intestines were swollen, and I had to be careful to eat only soft foods, but I knew God was with me," she reported. "He surrounded me with family and friends who prayed for me, encouraged me, and were so supportive."

Jehovah Rophe

> In this you greatly rejoice…that the genuineness of your faith, being much more precious than gold that perishes, though it is tested by fire, may be found to praise, honor, and glory at the revelation of Jesus Christ, whom having not seen you love. Though now you do not see Him, yet believing, you rejoice with joy inexpressible and full of glory.
>
> —1 PETER 1:6–8

I am the God who heals thee

She had a break for a few weeks of rest, then it was time to begin the second stage of treatment—a stronger form of chemotherapy. But during that period, Steven, Gaby's three-year-old, contracted chicken pox, and she had never had the childhood disease. When she reported this to her doctor, he told her it should pose no problem and persuaded her to continue the treatments on schedule.

"I agreed to this against my better judgment," Gaby said. "Looking back, I realize that God was warning me against taking the treatment, but I was just too weak to stand my ground. By the end of the second week I felt awful. I now had chicken pox and couldn't eat or drink anything because of horrible sores in my mouth and throat."

Very early one morning Gaby felt so sick that she awakened her husband. "Jeremy, I need help—I'm dehydrated," she told him. He took her to the hospital, where they hooked her up to IVs to rehydrate her, which helped her feel somewhat better. But when they did blood tests they discovered she had almost no white blood cells to protect her immune system. Her body went into shock because of the effects of chemotherapy, chicken pox, dehydration, plus a fungus and another infection that had developed. Her skin was dark and hardened, and sores covered her scalp.

The hospital kept her in isolation to protect her from disease, and the doctors warned Jeremy, who stayed with her constantly, that if she were to catch the flu she could die. He informed his parents daily about Gaby's condition, and they sent out e-mail requests to their prayer partners across Mexico and the United States, including me (Ruthanne). For six days she was kept alive with IVs, but she was not getting better.

JOY RESTORED

"The joy of the LORD is your strength" (Neh. 8:10) had always been one of Gaby's favorite scriptures. But in the crisis before her now, her joy was slipping away, and she became newly aware that she would have to fight to maintain it. Jeremy's strength helped her to keep believing that God would bring her through this.

Because of the sores in her mouth it was too painful to talk, and she couldn't even swallow her saliva, so she kept a small towel nearby to clean her mouth. When she wanted to communicate with Jeremy she would knock on the side of the bed to get his attention, then write him a note.

Late on the seventh night of being in isolation, she wrote to her husband, "Let's pray—I need a miracle tonight." Jeremy began to pray in tongues, and she was praying silently, asking God for a miracle.

"I understood the gift of tongues and had prayed to receive the Holy Spirit, but I had not yet spoken in tongues," she said. "One woman who had prayed with me some time before told me, 'God will give you tongues in a special way when you really need them.' While praying I looked down at the small towel I always kept with me, and strange words appeared there. But I couldn't recognize them—the writing was neither English nor Spanish."

She whispered to Jeremy, "Look, there are words on my towel," and held it up for him to see. But he saw nothing. "Just try to read the words out loud—don't worry about what they mean," he told her.

When Gaby began pronouncing the words aloud, she was suddenly speaking in tongues. All the pain left her mouth and throat, and she was able to speak and swallow freely. The room was filled with peace, and for the rest of the night she slept well for the first time in weeks.

"From that day, everything changed," she said. "The next morning I prayed and said, 'Thank You, Lord, for this miracle!' When I looked at my towel, I saw the word JOY in big letters. I began weeping as I suddenly felt the joy of the Lord just filling me up."

For the next five days Gaby drank a fortified milk drink for her meals, then began eating soft foods. As she continued getting stronger, her skin became normal, and at the end of the second week she returned home. One of her great thrills was being able to prepare a meal for her family again.

After one month her blood count and immune system were normal, so she completed the less stringent part of the chemotherapy and did fine with it. Almost a year after the first surgery, she returned to the hospital to have the colostomy removed. By now big clumps of her hair had fallen out, so she asked Jeremy to shave her head.

Jehovah Rophe

> Yet I will rejoice in the LORD,
> I will joy in the God of my salvation.
> The LORD God is my strength;
> He will make my feet like deer's feet,
> And He will make me walk on my high hills.
>
> —HABAKKUK 3:18–19

I am the God who heals thee

"I had so much to live for, I wasn't worried about losing my hair," she said. "Although the doctors told me I may never have hair again because of the shock to my system, I said, 'Not me—this is temporary.' I got some wigs, scarves, and hats and had fun with changing my looks from day to day. Sure enough, three months later my hair had grown back. It's still short, but it's thick and curly. The doctor was surprised, but I just said, 'I told you so!'"

Since she has only half a colon, doctors said she would have to follow a special diet and take a fiber product every day for the rest of her life. But that hasn't been necessary. She takes a juice vitamin supplement and eats anything she wants with no trouble—except now she's being a bit careful because she doesn't want to gain any more weight.

"The doctors also told me, 'No way can you have another baby,'" Gaby said. "But I reminded them that many of the things they said would happen haven't happened, and things they said could not happen did—such as my hair growing back. So I told them, 'You don't have the last word; God does. And I believe in miracles.'

"I am enjoying life and enjoying my son, and trusting God for His ways to give us more children, whether by birth or adoption.

I continue to thank God for surrounding me with people who encourage me. One Sunday at church a lady came and hugged me and said, 'I just can't stop crying since I heard what has happened.' But I told her, 'I don't need you to cry for me—that doesn't help me at all. Rejoice with me for my healing.'"

Jehovah Rophe

> To everything there is a season,
> A time for every purpose under heaven…
> A time to weep,
>   And a time to laugh;
> A time to mourn,
>   And a time to dance.
>
> —ECCLESIASTES 3:1, 4

I am the God who heals thee

The stress of a serious illness or sudden injury may cause you to feel depressed and anxious—a fairly normal human response. As we've just illustrated, the joy of the Lord is a powerful antidote against depression. However, in some cases depression may be caused by chemical imbalances or other physiological issues.

THE FOG OF DEPRESSION

Whether it is manic-depressive illness (bipolar), schizophrenia, eating disorders, attention-deficit hyperactivity disorder, anxiety disorders, or other maladies that affect our emotional and mental processes, the condition and pain are real. And the victims suffer. Their cries for healing are as real as the cries of those with cancer or any other illness. As a church body, we need to be better equipped to help those suffering with depression.

Martha Russell is a business woman who suffered with depression for some time, but she also struggled with feeling that church folks looked on her as though she had leprosy.

"Cancer is an enemy we can understand," she said. "Depression is a similar kind of enemy, but many people don't see it that way. They may easily reach out to pray for and support those stricken with cancer. But the perception is that Christians shouldn't be depressed—they are supposed to be joyful, hopeful people."

She should know as she has battled both depression and cancer and won over them both. And I (Quin) can attest that she is one of the most joyful women I have ever known.

When Martha was struggling with depression, she was embarrassed and ashamed of her condition, but in desperation, she finally sought help from a Christian doctor. "What is happening to you is not because of something you have done, or sin in your life, or because of a demon," he reassured her. "You have a chemical imbalance in your brain called 'bipolar 2.'"

She was glad to learn she was not a lazy, good-for-nothing individual who had brought this on herself because of poor choices in the past. Still, because of the stigma attached to such a disorder, it took her two months to acknowledge the fact that she had a mental illness.

In her own words, Martha tells the story of walking through the fog of depression.

----◆◆◆----

I had been on the verge of suicide when my friend Karen took me to a Christian psychiatrist, who put me on three medications: an antidepressant, a mood stabilizer, and a sleeping pill. When the doctor put a name—bipolar 2—on my condition I was greatly relieved. Karen and her husband took me into their home to live, and I became accountable to them, which proved to be a major factor in my healing.

When I first began taking the medications, they broke down the defense mechanisms I had devised in order to function every day, so the initial effects were negative. My motor skills became so impaired that I had couldn't hold a cup of coffee, dress myself, or even tie my shoes. My speech would get slurred. I couldn't feed myself, let alone cut up my food. I certainly couldn't drive a car. Many days I felt like a zombie.

But Karen's persistent care truly salvaged my life. She constantly played praise music in my room. Every day she would sit and read the Bible to me and administer Communion when I couldn't even hold the elements. She fed me, dressed me, and encouraged me to talk about my feelings. During those first few months, Karen devoted most of her time and energy to helping me get better, and she never made me feel put down. She read children's bedtime stories to help me relax at night. She'd see that I got adequate amounts of protein in my diet and that I spent at least an hour a day outdoors in the sunlight.

When I first tried to start attending church again I had panic attacks because of the noise and crowds. I believed strongly in healing. I also knew my hope was in God, not in the psychiatrist. But I was determined to be a good patient and follow my doctor's orders. I took the prescribed medications to control my depression and to make me sleep at night. I was also accountable to Karen, who kept a diary of my progress. I went up for healing prayers during altar ministry at church literally hundreds of times. I would sometimes see a slight improvement in my condition, but I was not healed.

One day I was in a service when a minister from Australia laid hands on me, looked me in the eye, and said, "Today, I agree with you for your healing." Instantly I began to laugh and cry at the same time. The word "today" gave me such hope. After he prayed for me, there was at last a settling in my spirit that I would be healed.

I continued to improve, and the doctor gradually decreased my dosages. Some five years after my initial diagnosis I was in church one day when I knew in my spirit it was time for no more medication. By now I was taking only half a dose of the antidepressant and was functioning adequately. With the assurance that I was healed, I decided not to take a sleeping pill that night, and I slept soundly. A week later I was still sleeping through the night with no medication, and I haven't taken any since. I knew that God had completed my healing.

Because I was accountable to Karen, I shared with her and another prayer partner that I felt I was now healed and could cease taking the medications. After prayer they came into agreement with my decision. But had I lapsed into irrational behavior at any time, they would have confronted me. That was more than two years ago, and I have had no more symptoms.

Restore to me the joy of Your salvation,
And uphold me by Your generous Spirit....

Those who sow in tears
Shall reap in joy.

—PSALMS 51:12; 126:5

The prayer that most often came from Martha's lips was, "Restore my soul…O God, please restore my soul." And He did. She says her healing was progressive as she kept trusting God step-by-step for complete restoration. Today she owns her own home and enjoys her work at her business that she and Karen operate together. She also has an interest in Israel and makes frequent trips there.

WHAT IS BIPOLAR DISORDER?

Bipolar disorder, also known as manic-depressive illness, is a brain disorder that causes unusual shifts in a person's mood, energy, and ability to function. The person goes from periods (or episodes) of mania to depression.[3]

During a manic episode, persons with bipolar disorder may exhibit a higher than normal energy level, little need for sleep, poor judgment, increased sexual drive, and provocative or aggressive behavior. They are more likely to abuse drugs, alcohol, and sleeping medications, and they often deny that anything is wrong.

During a depressed phase, patients may experience persistent sadness, hopelessness and pessimism, loss of appetite, loss of interest in activities that were once enjoyed, sleep disturbances, thoughts of death and suicide, withdrawal, fatigue, feelings of guilt, and difficulty remembering or making decisions.[4]

While we know we are composed of body, soul, and spirit, when a person's soul or emotions are sick, society in general tends to attach a certain stigma to him or her. Sadly, that attitude is often found within the church also. Bipolar disorder, for instance, sees an affected person's moods swing from excessive highs (mania) to profound hopelessness (depression), often with periods of normal mood in between.

Martha and countless others who are victors over depression have learned to focus on one day at a time, trusting God for strength and guidance for just that day. If you are fighting depression, following these steps can help steer you toward victory:

- Recovery begins by recognizing you have a problem and seeking help.

- Renew your mind with truth.

- Change your false beliefs about yourself and your situation.

- Ask God to show you ways to reduce the stress factors in your life and to resist the deception the enemy tries to bring to your mind.

- Don't live in isolation—seek help from family or friends who are willing to help bear your burden.

- Believe in yourself. God made you in His image, and you are precious to Him.

- Ask God to replace your sorrow with His joy.

- Meditate on the Scriptures; if reading is difficult, play audio recordings of Scripture or praise music.

- Remember the promise: "I can do all things through Him who strengthens me" (Phil. 4:13, NAS).

LAUGHTER CAN AID IN HEALING

The Bible says laughter is good medicine. Why? When we laugh, endorphins, the "feel good" hormones, can produce an energy boost. Dr. Don Colbert has said that the diaphragm, thorax, abdomen, heart, lungs, and liver are given a massage during a hearty laugh.[5]

Other studies have shown that if we cry when we laugh, those tears may reduce symptoms of stress. Loma Linda professor Dr. Lee Berk and others have tested the saliva of patients after laughing episodes and found that they have higher levels of disease-fighting agents called immunoglobulins. Other studies suggest that laughter may raise our immune function. A hearty laugh can be as beneficial as exercising.[6]

Joy is mentioned 158 times and *laugh* or *laughter* over two dozen times in the Bible. What is this joy the Bible speaks about? One definition is "a quiet, inner sense of well-being." But it can also mean "to spin around, rejoice, be glad, be joyful."[7]

How in the world can we rejoice or be glad when we are sick? By calling upon the Holy Spirit to help us look beyond our current distress and concentrating on God's character, goodness, faithfulness, promises, and provisions.

The scripture at the beginning of this chapter is the one Jesus read in the synagogue at Nazareth affirming His own ministry (Luke 4:18). Among other things, He came "to give them...the oil of joy for mourning, the garment of praise for the spirit of heaviness" (Isa. 61:3). One commentator provides this insight:

> The Hebrew root for "garment" shows praise as more than a piece of clothing casually thrown over our shoulders. It literally teaches us "to wrap" or "cover" ourselves—that the garment of praise is to leave no openings through which hostile elements can penetrate. This garment of praise repels and replaces the heavy spirit.[8]

Ruth Myers writes:

> Through praise you focus your attention on God. You acknowledge Him as your source of overcoming power. You begin to look at your problems from a new perspective—you compare them with your mighty, unlimited God....You have a part in making them the prelude to new victories, the raw materials for God's miracles.[9]

As we learn to praise God for who He is, we will see how much easier it is to ask Him to restore our relationships—a subject we will explore in our next chapter.

Now let's find some things for which to be joyful as we pray.

PRAYER

Lord, I choose to be joyful simply because You are trustworthy. Dear Jesus, I praise You no matter how I feel: for Your salvation, for Your provision, for my family and friends, for my medical helpers, for the blessings in my life thus far (name other things to praise Him for). *Clothe me with a garment of praise every time I feel heaviness and discouragement pressing in on me. Help me to look up and know that there is joy in each day, there is gladness in knowing You. You are indeed my strength and my salvation. Thank You, Lord. Amen.*

Restoration in every dimension of human experience is at the heart of the Christian gospel.... Acts 3:19–21 makes the most pointed reference to restoration in the New Testament. Peter urges a return to God for cleansing from sins. He adds that this returning would pave the way for a period of refreshing renewal that would result from the presence of the Lord with His people.

...When something is restored in the Scriptures, it is always increased, multiplied or improved, so that its latter state is significantly better than its original state (see Joel 2:21–26).[1]

—*James Robison*

8

Lord,

RESTORE MY RELATIONSHIPS

Repent therefore and be converted, that your sins may be blotted out, so that times of refreshing may come from the presence of the Lord, and that He may send Jesus Christ, who was preached to you before, whom heaven must receive until the times of restoration of all things.

—ACTS 3:19–21

NOT ALL SICK people are wrapped in the arms of love and care. Some have been estranged from family members or former friends for some time, yet God often moves in unexpected ways to restore those broken relationships.

- When a drug-addicted woman is finally healed, she regains custody of her son.

- A man who lived several years beyond what doctors predicted mended connections with family members willing to make things right between them.

- Another who wanted nothing to do with God was reconciled both to his Creator and to his family after undergoing emergency surgery.

Many of us can probably name people we know who experienced some measure of reconciliation with loved ones as a result of a serious illness or accident. We want to look now at biblical and contemporary examples of restoration.

Clearly, restoration has been God's plan since man's fall, as Jesus' earthly ministry illustrates. One biblical definition of "to restore" includes returning to a former condition of health, such as when a man with a withered hand was brought to Jesus and "it was restored as whole as the other" (Matt. 12:13; also see Mark 3:5; 8:25; Luke 6:10).[2]

To restore can also mean to mend. For example, in Galatians 6:1: "Brethren, if a man is overtaken in any trespass, you who are spiritual restore such a one in a spirit of gentleness, considering yourself lest you also be tempted." Here, the Greek word used for "restore" was the secular term used for setting broken bones.[3]

Jehovah Rophe

And the God of all grace, who called you to his eternal glory in Christ, after you have suffered a little while, will himself restore you and make you strong, firm and steadfast. To him be the power for ever and ever. Amen.

—1 PETER 5:10–11, NIV

I am the God who heals thee

The Bible has much to say about our relationships with one another in passages sometimes referred to as "reciprocal commands." Some are: love one another, pray for one another, bear one another's burdens, forgive one another, comfort one another, accept one another, confess your sins to one another, don't judge one another, encourage one another, be kind to one another, be hospitable to one another. And on and on they go.*

God is the source of the "one anothers." We love because He first loved us, but God wants to use us as His hands extended here on earth. We need each other, especially when we are sick or serving as caregiver for an ill person.

The following story is of a man who was restored to his heavenly Father as well as to his earthly family. But it only happened when his sister-in-law first repented, then rallied others to action.

GAINING SPIRITUAL VISION

Lillie** cringed every time she heard Robert** hurl angry, abusive words at his wife, her younger sister. She and her other siblings often criticized him to one another. "Did you see what he did? Did you hear what he called her? He makes Sister's life hell on earth."

One day the Lord convicted Lillie by impressing her with this thought: *If you spent as much time praying for him as you do criticizing him, I could have done more in his life by now.* Immediately she recognized her sin of judging and asked God's forgiveness. Then she called her family members together and asked them to commit to pray for him regularly. Right then they had a corporate prayer meeting, and several other such sessions followed. Their constant request: for Robert to have a change of

---

* See Ephesians 5:21; Colossians 3:9, 13, 16; 1 Thessalonians 3:12; 5:11; Hebrews 3:13; 10:24–25; 1 Peter 4:9–10.
** Name changed for privacy

heart by accepting Jesus as his Lord.

Three years later he had a heart attack and was rushed to the surgical ward for emergency open-heart surgery. Doctors offered little hope for his recovery. As Lillie sat in the waiting room with family members, she was reading her Bible when this verse seemed to leap up at her. It was God speaking:

> I hid my face and was angry, and he went on turning away and backsliding in the way of his [own willful] heart. I have seen his [willful] ways, but I will heal him; I will lead him also and will recompense him and restore comfort to him and to those who mourn for him.
>
> —Isaiah 57:17–18, amp

God's peace fell like a blanket across her. She was assured God was doing something wonderful for her brother-in-law.

Robert remained in a coma for three weeks, unresponsive to anyone. Then one day he opened his eyes. But he couldn't see. He was blind.

Yet something miraculous had happened to his heart. During those three weeks he'd had an encounter with the Lord. Now instead of lashing out, kindness was in his voice. "I have a lot to make right…I saw the Lord," he told his wife one day without elaborating.

When they moved him to a hospital bed at home, people immediately noticed that he smiled instead of frowned. He was now a grateful, caring, compassionate man; belligerence was no longer on his tongue. God had indeed changed his heart in response to his family's prayers.

His wife's pastor made regular visits to his bedside, praying and reading Scripture to him. Robert, who would never go to church, let alone allow a pastor to visit him, now had a pastor whom he grew to love.

"He went into surgery with physical eyes and then lost his eyesight, but he came out with spiritual vision," Lillie explained. "He also had a spiritual heart healing, if not a permanent physical one." When Robert died some months later, his pastor offered his family and friends comfort as he spoke about the remarkable turnaround this man had experienced in coming to know the Lord.

Sometimes the Lord may arrest our attention and change our own attitudes, as He did for Lillie. But always, if we ask, He will guide us in how to specifically focus our prayer efforts for the one we are concerned about. And in the process we shouldn't be surprised if damaged relationships are repaired.

ANOTHER FAMILY RELATIONSHIP RESTORED

The late Judson Cornwall, a renowned Charismatic teacher and preacher, was amazingly transparent in his excellent book *Dying With Grace* as he shared about his three-year journey with cancer.

While his suffering and pain were very real, he experienced some of his greatest joys by seeing several family relationships restored. For instance, his grandson David came from Atlanta with his estranged wife and their three-year-old son to visit Grandpa. As they stood beside his bed talking, little Jon Jon crawled up in bed with his great-grandpa and fell asleep.

Judson said this incident played a major role in causing the couple to take another look at their lives, and they decided to remarry.

> *Jehovah Rophe*
>
> Now all things are of God, who has reconciled us to Himself through Jesus Christ, and has given us the ministry of reconciliation.
>
> —2 CORINTHIANS 5:18
>
> *I am the God who heals thee*

One night Judson awoke and announced to his wife that he was bringing David's family to Phoenix to live near them. Within a short time a house was purchased, and they moved just a block away from David's mother's house. When they got settled, their home was the setting for the marriage of David's mom, with Judson conducting the ceremony from a lounge chair.

He wrote, "Would the couple's marriage have been salvaged if I had gone home to glory as rapidly as the doctors predicted? I don't know. I just know that God wanted to use me as a catalyst to rescue a couple to whom God had imparted a gift of hospitality. It has been worth the extra pain I have had to endure to remain here."

He tells of many other relationship "joys" he was thankful to God for allowing him to experience, even from his bed—including a closer bond with his wife.[4]

RESTORING DISEASED BONES AND BROKEN RELATIONSHIPS

God wants to restore broken health as well as damaged relationships, and this actually happened in Terri Lugenheim's family. She shares her painfully honest journey that she believes led to her son's healing and the restoration of her troubled marriage. In her own words:

Several years ago, when I began to notice that my nine-year-old son Christian was limping noticeably and one of his legs was thinner than the other, I took him for a checkup. After a series of several X-rays and appointments with different specialists, he was diagnosed with Legg-Calve-Perthes disease, a slow disintegration of the top portion of the femur head due to a lack of blood flow. This rare disease is named for the three doctors who discovered it. In some cases, children with this problem grow up having to use arm crutches or walk with a terrible limp. Many suffer from arthritis or have to undergo complete hip replacements in adulthood.

My heart was flooded with fear and doubt when I got the doctor's report. I cried out to God to heal my son, but nothing happened. After a while I began to question my faith. "If God promised to heal all our diseases (Ps. 103:3), then why wasn't my son healed?" Weeks of prayer and many trips to the doctor culminated in Christian having surgery. He suffered much pain, and it was also painful for me to listen to his screams. He was in a body cast from the waist down for four weeks after surgery, and I home-schooled him during this time. Physicians gave us hope for only a possible 30 percent recovery.

Although I'm a Christian and love God with all my heart, after eleven years of marriage and three children plus three miscarriages, I found myself imprisoned in a self-made hell. I had spent most of those years in unforgiveness, hurt by an accumulation of things my husband had said and done to me. Our marriage had begun to fall apart, and my second son started having asthma attacks. Our entire family was miserable, and the devil was having a free-for-all. Yet we seemed powerless to do anything about it, regardless of how hard we prayed.

Then one day, still searching for answers to my desperation, I heard a teaching tape based on the parable about the unforgiving servant. The story concludes:

> Then his master, after he had called him, said to him, "You wicked servant! I forgave you all that debt because you begged me. Should you not also have had compassion on your fellow servant, just as I had pity on you?" And his master was angry, and delivered him to the torturers until he should pay all that was due to him. So My heavenly Father also will do to you if each of you, from his heart, does not forgive his brother his trespasses.
> —MATTHEW 18:32–34

The Lord gave me a vision of my husband behind bars—the bars of unforgiveness. And the reflection of the "wicked servant" in the mirror of those scriptures was *me*! Jesus was saying that we will receive forgiveness "in the same way" we forgive others. I realized that I had been turned over to the tormentors in various areas of my life because I was unwilling to forgive. I read the last verse again: "So My heavenly Father also will do to you if each of you, from his heart, does not forgive his brother his trespasses." My spirit was grieved.

The Lord dealt mightily with my heart, and what seemed to be the impossible task of forgiving suddenly became easy. I realized that forgiveness was a decision. It had nothing to do with any wrong done or the feelings I nurtured about it. That very night, I went to my husband and repented of my unforgiveness. I told him that I forgave him, that I loved him, and that there was nothing that could happen to cause me to walk in unforgiveness again. As I refused to give place to the devil in my life or the life of my family members, God began to restore our marriage.

I prayed diligently for my husband to be blessed and placed a prayer cloth under his pillow. In the mornings, while making the bed, I'd take the cloth out, pray scriptures over it, and then place it back in his pillowcase.

Jehovah Rophe

Create in me a clean heart, O God,
And renew a steadfast spirit within me.
Do not cast me away from Your presence,
And do not take Your Holy Spirit from me.
Restore to me the joy of Your salvation,
And uphold me by Your generous Spirit.
Then I will teach transgressors Your ways,
And sinners shall be converted to you.
—PSALM 51:10–12

I am the God who heals thee

As I sought the Lord with a heart of obedience, He started moving in powerful ways within our family. My middle son Caleb was healed of asthma, and daily our marriage was being restored.

Yet, our son Christian's health struggles continued. Now his other hip had developed the same disease, and doctors wanted to operate. The disease had stunted his bone growth, and he was losing weight. It had come down to this: we had to choose whose report we were going to believe. Either we believed the doctors and opted for yet another difficult surgery, or we would stand on the Word of God and believe for Christian's total healing.

One day I was reading Isaiah 53:1–5, when I felt the Lord instructed me to undertake a forty-day fast. He had been preparing me for this for several months. Together, my husband and I claimed that "by His stripes we are healed," and I started a liquids-only fast.

About thirty days into the fast the Lord dealt with me about submission to my husband. I began to weep. That day I took practical steps toward becoming a more submissive wife. I asked my husband's advice about different issues, and I made a more concerted effort to accomplish things with the children that he had asked me to do. My view of him began to change, and I saw him become gentler with the children and less critical of me.

Shortly after I completed my fast, X-rays from yet another doctor's appointment showed that Christian's hip was healing nicely without the prescribed surgery. In fact, at our last appointment in the summer of 2005, the doctor said to Christian, "You are perfect."

My son Caleb was completely healed of asthma and has not had an attack in more than two years. My marriage has been transformed into a peaceful one, and I love my husband more than ever before. The tormentors no longer have legal right over my family as I walk in obedience to God's Word. It is true: Nothing is impossible with God!

Terri became a key intercessor in her church's "healing room," where about forty people a week are prayed for during the times it is open for healing prayers. She has seen many miracles take place through this ministry. Terri told me (Quin) that she believes her own heart-change led to the healing of both sons, as well as to the healing of her marriage.

God works in mysterious ways to accomplish His purposes, and that includes restoring relationships and healing disintegrating bones. As we have seen throughout this book, the Lord deals with each of us differently, and there are no "formulas" that necessarily guarantee a healing. We cannot box Him in with our own timetable and expectation of how He will accomplish His purpose. But thankfully, the Lord speaks to us so that we can understand. When we respond with obedience, He is always willing to intervene in ways that bring Him glory and honor.

Our next story concerns a man who could have missed the greatest relationship decision of his life. In fact, he might have even missed heaven had he not made a critical decision as he lay in a hospital bed after a near-fatal accident.

HIS RELATIONSHIP WITH JESUS SECURED

Late on the last night of July in 2002, Michelle and Mike Novotny departed from their home in northern California en route to Mike's new military assignment in Oklahoma. As they headed across the Mojave Desert, a little past four in the morning, Mike fell asleep at the wheel of their Jeep Cherokee.

The rough movements of the car awakened Michelle, and she heard Mike yell, "Oh, no! Oh, no!" She also heard a still, small voice saying, *"Keep your eyes closed and stay focused on Me."* So she called out, "O Lord Jesus, O Lord Jesus," until their Jeep finally quit rolling over and over.

I am the God who heals thee

Their car stopped upside down, with Mike and Michelle suspended by their seatbelts. Michelle managed to get out of her seatbelt and out of the vehicle, while Mike was still trapped.

Mike remembers feeling helpless and in pain, then without a conscious effort on his part, he suddenly felt his neck bend back. This gave him just the room he needed to reach over with his right arm, freeing his left arm, which was pinned under the bent steering wheel.

Sometime after Michelle's escape, while Mike was still trapped, a trucker stopped when he saw the Jeep in the median only ten feet from the westbound lane. Mike and Michelle had been heading east! The trucker called 9-1-1, and several emergency vehicles and personnel arrived within five minutes of each other.

Mike and Michelle were both placed on backboards, and they braced Mike with a collar because he complained of constant neck pain. The medics rushed them to a hospital in Lancaster, California.

Michelle had a broken right shoulder blade, a large lump was on the right side of her head, and several lacerations on her feet, arms, and back. But Mike had a broken neck and was listed in critical condition. The neurosurgeon said Mike had a "burst fracture" to the C-7 vertebra and recommended immediate surgery. But he warned of three possible results: he might not survive the operation, he might come out paralyzed, or he could become fully mobile.

The doctor, who was shocked when he learned what they had gone through to get out of the upside-down vehicle, warned Mike not to move at all. According to Michelle, Mike was not only stiff because he had to remain still, but he was literally scared stiff.

Michelle felt a nudge from the Holy Spirit to ask Mike if he remembered the e-mails they had sent back and forth during the time he was deployed in the initial response to the 9/11 terrorist attacks. In those e-mails she had told him how to receive the Lord, since she herself had rededicated her own life a few years earlier. In one message she asked him the question someone had once asked her: "Can you think of any good reason why not to ask Jesus into your heart?"

Now when Michelle asked Mike in the hospital emergency room if he had ever asked Jesus to become his personal Lord and Savior, he said, "No." Then he bellowed out, "But I want to do that right now."

So on August 1, 2002, Michelle led her husband in what she called "the sinner's prayer of faith." After Mike asked Jesus into his heart, Michelle explained to him that he was now a child of God. That no matter whether God chose to take him now on the operating table or to let him live on this earth longer, Mike would always be a part of the kingdom of God.

She then prayed for the Holy Spirit to comfort Mike and for God to guide the surgeon's hands. Mike was visibly relaxed, no longer rigid with fear. He told Michelle that he was not afraid at all when he was rolled into the operating room.

Jehovah Rophe

"Now, therefore," says the LORD,
"Turn to Me with all your heart,
With fasting, with weeping, and with mourning.
So rend your heart, and not your garments;
Return to the LORD your God,
For He is gracious and merciful,
Slow to anger, and of great kindness;
And He relents from doing harm....
So I will restore to you the years that the swarming locust
has eaten."

—JOEL 2:12–13, 25

I am the God who heals thee

The doctor later explained to them that Mike's spine was only one-eighth of an inch from being severed. But amazingly, he was up and out of bed only two days after surgery and released from the hospital in five days.

One month after the accident, Mike's relatives drove them to Oklahoma for his military assignment. While Mike was on convalescent leave for another month, they became active in a local church. Mike was baptized in water as a public affirmation of his faith shortly after his doctor released him back to full duty. Three months after the accident he received healing of one of his vocal cords, which had been paralyzed during surgery to his neck. He is grateful to the members of their new church for prayers concerning that miracle.

When Mike went to a neurosurgeon for a six-month checkup, complete with X-rays of his neck, the doctor told him his neck had healed so well that only the best-trained eye could tell there had ever been a fracture.

"I prayed for four years for Mike's salvation and finally stopped worrying but thanked God for doing this in His timing," Michelle said. "I was putting my faith in God that He would eventually answer my prayer as my heart's desire lined up with God's desire. I then started praying for the privilege of being able to know that Mike was saved." Hebrews 4:16 is a verse that has become precious to her: "Let us therefore come boldly to the throne of grace, that we may obtain mercy and find grace to help in time of need."

She feels that when she called upon Jesus at the moment of their accident, she came boldly before God's throne of grace. "Mike and I received mercy and grace, helping us in our greatest time of need," she said. As of this writing, they live in Anchorage, Alaska, for a two-year tour where Mike is a squadron commander responsible for more than 350 people who maintain three different types of aircraft.

Not only did Mike's miracle of healing give him a second chance at life on earth, but he now has the assurance of spending eternity with the God who created him. All because he made that quality decision for "relationship" during his crisis moment. Added to that is the joy of a new relationship with his wife and with fellow members of the body of Christ.

JESUS, A MAN OF COMPASSION

The Jewish people mostly believed that sickness was the direct consequence of sin resulting in God's judgment. However, Jesus showed a forgiving, compassionate side. In the healing of a blind man who had been sick since birth, He said the sickness was not related to the sins of the man or his father, but it was for God's glory. (See John 9:1–4.)

When a nobleman heard that Jesus had come into Galilee, he went to implore Him to come heal his son who was at the point of death in Capernaum. Jesus said to him, "Go your way; your son lives" (John 4:50). The man believed the words Jesus spoke to him. As he returned home, his servants met him with good news: "Your son lives!" (v. 51). The father learned that the fever left at the exact hour Jesus had pronounced life over his son.

Look at the "relationship" results of this healing: not only did the man believe in Jesus, but his whole household did as well—all those related to the sick lad. Just imagine the excited sharing that went on among those who saw or heard about this miraculous healing. So it is with us when we share with others an answer to prayer and express our faith in Christ's life-giving power.

Jesus definitely is in the restoration and renewal business. And He wants to help us in building meaningful relationships with our family members and fellow believers. True, this may come after time spent in repentance, and perhaps during a health crisis. But what joyful refreshing comes when we see the fruit of obeying God's instructions to us.

In the following chapter we will look into ways to take advantage of these restored relationships as we encourage one another.

PRAYER

Lord, thank You that You are a God of restoration—both of body and soul. Thank You that You care deeply about me having healthy, wholesome relationships. Please bring the people of Your choice into my life to accomplish Your will during this season of my life. May I in turn be sensitive to reach out to those with whom I need to be in closer relationship. Forgive me for the times I have not been obedient—when I judged or criticized and didn't choose to forgive. Lord, give me strength and wisdom in those areas where I'm lacking, and I will give You the thanks and glory. Amen.

Whether you are blessed with soul mates who settled into the most comfortable room inside you, or with those who walk with you just a little while, not one of these people crosses your path by chance. Each is a messenger, sent by God, to give you the wisdom, companionship, comfort, or challenge you need for a particular leg of your spiritual journey.[1]

—*Traci Mullins and Ann Spangler*

9

Lord,
MAKE ME AN ENCOURAGER

Encourage the exhausted, and strengthen the feeble.
Say to those with anxious heart,
"Take courage, fear not."

—ISAIAH 35:3–4, NAS

GOD HAS CALLED us to be encouragers. If God has brought you through a horrendous illness or accident, you're in a unique position to say honestly to a suffering friend, "I can empathize with you—I've been there. Here, let me help you walk through it." Or you may be blessed to be on the receiving end of such help.

The Lord often uses the prayers and encouragement of others as the catalyst to bring healing in our lives. In this chapter we share examples of people who have been healed through the believing prayers of a minister, a prayer group, or friends and family members. We also give helpful ways to encourage the sick and their families.

STANDING ON THE WORD

Sherry Grace Anderson was desperate for answers after learning she was suffering from a blood disease for which there was no medication to ease the symptoms. One night, out of curiosity, she attended a tent revival on the edge of town. When the minister declared that the miracles of the Bible are available today, just as when Jesus walked the earth, it challenged her personal beliefs. But she was willing to explore the Scriptures, even though her church did not embrace this theology. She tells us about her disease and about her encounter with the Lord:

--------◆◆◆◆◆--------

At first I didn't know what was wrong. Depression, crying spells, headaches, and muscle fatigue were all plaguing me. Through medical tests I was diagnosed with spontaneous reactive hypoglycemia, which is the opposite of diabetes. My doctor said there was no cure, and the only treatment was a low-carbohydrate diet. I could eat no sweets, and only one serving of a carbohydrate at a time—such as only one piece of bread. I simply had to learn to live with the problem.

During my prayer time one day I told the Lord, "You said all things work together for good. What good has come out of this?" Several things came to mind: discipline in my life, learning about nutrition, and compassion for others who were ill. Then I went to a tent revival where, for the first time, I heard this scripture read, referring to Jesus Christ:

He was despised and rejected by men, a man of sorrows, and familiar with suffering....Surely he took up our infirmities and carried our sorrows, yet we considered him stricken by God, smitten by him, and afflicted. But he was pierced for our transgressions, he was crushed for our iniquities; the punishment that brought us peace was upon him, and by his wounds we are healed.

—Isaiah 53:3–5, niv

I knew the first part of the passage was true because Jesus died for me and I had received Him as my Savior three years earlier. So I decided if I was going to believe the first verses of this chapter, that I would believe the rest of it! During the altar call I went forward for prayer. The minister prayed for my healing, and in faith I received it. "Now thank God for your healing," he said.

I felt a little awkward. How do you thank someone for healing an incurable disease? I just said, "Thank You, Lord," over and over. My words felt so small in comparison to the blessing!

I knew the Word of God was true. And when I was prayed for I embraced that truth, so that settled it for me. However, the symptoms persisted. As a matter of fact, it took nearly a year for the healing to completely manifest. During that year I stood on this confession: "By His stripes (wounds) we are healed."

Not only did I have to fight for the healing, but I also have stood my ground to keep my healing over the past twenty-eight years. There were times when I would have a twinge of pain in my pancreas or exhibit other symptoms, and I'd feel my blood sugar was going way down. Immediately I'd say aloud, "By His stripes I am healed. Jesus did it for me, and I am not giving in!"

The pain or drowsiness would leave. Finally, the enemy quit bringing symptoms. Today I can eat anything I want without any side effects. But healing wasn't the only gift I received at that tent revival. Before the week was over I was also blessed with the baptism of the Holy Spirit and a prayer language. You can believe those gifts from God changed my theology and my life in dramatic ways! I am so thankful that "Jesus Christ is the same yesterday, today, and forever" (Heb. 13:8).

Today Sherry Grace is a teacher and author who instructs believers on how to stand effectively against the enemy's tactics through prayer and spiritual warfare. Because of her own firsthand experience, she's a great encouragement to those seeking God for healing who need a deeper understanding of Scripture.

Expecting Something

Can ordinary people perform extraordinary acts aided by God? Sherry Grace's miracle came after a minister prayed for her and she stood on the Word to claim supernatural healing. The Bible gives accounts of those who did do extraordinary acts, and God's power is still available today.

Jehovah Rophe

I will bless the LORD at all times;
His praise shall continually be in my mouth.
My soul shall make its boast in the LORD;
The humble shall hear of it and be glad.
Oh, magnify the LORD with me,
And let us exalt His name together.

—PSALM 34:1–3

I am the God who heals thee

Peter and John, on their way to the temple to pray at three o'clock one afternoon, encounter a man begging beside the temple gate called Beautiful. He has been a hopeless cripple his entire life.

"Look at us," Peter instructs as he and John stop and look intently at the man.

The man gives them his full attention, expecting to receive a few coins. But he gets far more than he expected!

"Silver and gold I do not have, but what I do have I give you," Peter tells him. "In the name of Jesus Christ of Nazareth, rise up and walk." Taking him by the right hand, he pulls him up, and instantly the man's ankles become strong and he begins to walk. He continues walking and leaping and praising God as he follows Peter and John into the temple area. The people recognize him as the same man who used to sit begging at the temple gate and are totally amazed. (See Acts 3:1–11.)

A crowd gathers, so Peter takes the opportunity to proclaim the message of salvation and healing through the power of Christ. Greatly disturbed, the authorities want to know by what power they have done this.

Peter, filled with Holy Spirit boldness, replies, "By the name of Jesus Christ of Nazareth, this man stands here before you whole." (See Acts 3:12–4:14.)

The authorities are clearly puzzled. After all, Peter and John are uneducated and untrained men—quite ordinary, really. But the leaders take note that these men had been with Jesus. Obviously, this is the key to the miracle.

From this one event, more than five thousand people believed on the Lord that day (Acts 4:4). And still today those who know Christ intimately, who are committed to prayer, who know the Scriptures, and who believe miracles have not ceased know how to exercise such New Testament faith.

It's one thing to believe God can heal a physical illness or mend broken or crippled bones. But can God do a creative miracle by providing a body part where it had never existed before? Such miracles are not common, although we have heard reports of this happening—most often in healing revivals outside the United States. However, in our next story you will read of a "creative miracle" achieved through modern surgery.

AN ENCOURAGER TO MANY

A baby girl delivered by C-section had no bladder and just one kidney, which was only 25 percent functional. Her left arm was missing a radial bone, causing her hand to twist and rendering her thumb useless. Also, she needed immediate surgery to connect her esophagus to her stomach. Then another surgery was performed to close an aortic defect that was causing her lungs to fill with blood. This is how Kaley Stuart entered the world.

Her condition, known as Vater Syndrome, is extremely rare and does not have a proven scientific cause, according to her dad, Chris. But a person with this condition can have multiple congenital anomalies. Could Kaley even survive? Chances of that possibility looked slim indeed, but doctors immediately connected her to life-support machines.

As the newborn's life was challenged, her grandmother Elizabeth rallied intercessors across the nation. Prayer teams prayed for her through every crisis, one surgery after another, and in between.

Jehovah Rophe

Now may the God who gives perseverance and encouragement grant you to be of the same mind with one another according to Christ Jesus; that with one accord you may with one voice glorify the God and Father of our Lord Jesus Christ.

—ROMANS 15:5–6, NAS

I am the God who heals thee

Once when she was just two and a half, I (Quin) was speaking in the city where her grandmother lived. Kaley was in the hospital

152

facing another life-threatening situation. Her surgically repaired esophagus was causing severe reflux that resulted in intense vomiting every time she ate. My prayer partner and I joined her grandmother in praying over Kaley. I knew it would take a miracle of God to save her, but that's what we prayed for.

Somehow she managed to survive, but her immune system was so fragile that when any germs or bacteria attacked her, she went back to the hospital. She was on a feeding machine most of her first three years of life, even while at home. Nevertheless, she had a strong will to live—plus a fighting spirit and a praying grandmother who talked to her constantly about God's love and purpose for her life.

Because Kaley had no bladder, she had to wear an external urostomy bag. It was cumbersome and many times would leak, embarrassing her. But she never whined or complained. The spunky little girl gained strength and agility by taking gymnastics, and she could turn cartwheels with the best of them. She became a strong swimmer and athlete along with being a fantastic student. Her beautiful voice won her first prize when she sang a solo in her school's Passion Play. Almost a normal kid, you might say.

Yet her "anatomical complications" were so great that when she was turning twelve, doctors began planning for two major surgeries that would help give her a more normal life. First, to create a bladder from a section of her stomach and a piece of her bowel. Second, to transplant a kidney from her father. That was the gigantic task awaiting her team of doctors at the Cincinnati Children's Hospital. Only a handful of surgical teams have experience in transplanting a kidney and connecting it to an augmented bladder. However, this hospital's team had performed twenty such procedures—the most among hospitals that do these surgeries, according to her dad.

Scripture Prayers of Encouragement

Prior to the surgery, her grandmother Elizabeth sent out dozens of prayer letters with a picture of Kaley, along with cards addressed to her. Each intercessor was to write on the card a scripture she would pray for this special child. Then Kaley would pray it over herself when she received the card. She took all those scripture cards with her to the hospital in a file box. Students at her Christian school prayed over her before she left, and dozens of friends stood by the parents and grandparents in the hospital waiting room.

The first surgery was very intense, lasting almost thirteen hours as doctors made a bladder out of her own organs. She was in intensive care for three weeks, with only one family member at a time able to see her. Round-the-clock nurses tended to her during her two-month hospital stay. "We all love it when we are assigned to Kaley because she's such an inspiration," one nurse said fondly. Many tubes were kept running into her body to help stave off infections and keep her stable.

Seven months later she underwent the second surgery, receiving one of her dad's kidneys, which was a perfect match. While she was recuperating, members of the football team from a state university visited with Kaley, having pictures made with her and making her feel special—a tiny girl among those giant men. When the local news captured the event and televised it on the evening newscast, she became something of a hero.

Today, at thirteen, Kaley is in the seventh grade and is thrilled that she's been chosen for the junior varsity cheerleading squad. She has a gift with words and shows great leadership ability. But mainly she is an encourager who lights up a room when she walks in—always reaching out to show appreciation and sensitivity for others.

"She is uninhibited and never meets a stranger," says her grandmother, who believes God spared her life so that she could encourage others. Recently she almost stole the show when she read from Corinthians at her uncle's wedding.

Since her case is so unusual and she has done so well, the doctors have taken her twice to meet with medical students and interns. She is very articulate, knows all the medical terms for her condition, and is open for them to question her. Since the kidney transplant, which contributes to normal growth, she has gained some weight and grown taller.

Her dad, Chris, and mother, Patty, have been her greatest supporters. Patty has stayed by her side constantly and has become an expert on Kaley's complicated medical condition.

When asked what part God played in her healing, Kaley's face lit up. "Oh, He was involved from the beginning," she said. "Such as having me in a hospital close to home where a top-notch team of specially trained doctors were available not only to operate but to care for me 24/7 if needed. I had wonderful nurses and my very own tutor. How easy God made it for me, and I am so thankful."

So we come back to the question: Can God do a creative miracle? Well, of course we know that God has all power in heaven and in earth, so yes, He can do anything. In Kaley's situation, God responded to prayer by providing the needed body parts through surgery.

In contrast to Kaley's case, the man in our next story received a creative miracle in response to prayer, so that surgery was not even necessary.

HEALED WITHOUT SURGERY

Bob Terhune's love for the "Wild West" and competing in rodeos led him to a forty-five-year career as a movie stunt man in California. But in 1962 a freak accident almost cost him that career.

Just six months before the accident, Bob had been filled with the Holy Spirit and had seen God do many signs and wonders in meetings at his sister's home. He now knew the real Healer. On that near-fateful day, he was on horseback doing a movie scene for the western series *Rawhide*, doubling for the main character.

Handing him a double-barreled shotgun loaded with "blank bullets," the assistant director asked him to start a cattle stampede. Bob hung the shotgun by the sling over his saddle horn and stood up in the stirrups to position himself. But as he jerked on the saddle, the gun suddenly discharged a full load of the twelve-gauge shots, hitting him in the face. Most of the shots targeted his left eye.

With his face covered with grease, dirt, and powder marks, he was rushed to the hospital, where one of the best eye specialists in all of Southern California examined him. The cornea in his left eye was in shreds, like cheese when it is grated. The eyeball, which was torn loose from the retina, was also ruptured and hemorrhaging.

"You will never see out of this eye," the doctor said as he swabbed it with ether.

"But doctor, the Lord is going to heal my eye," Bob replied.

Every time the doctor told him he'd never see out of that eye, Bob would say again, "The Lord is going to heal me! You do what you have to do, doctor, and the Lord will take care of the rest. My church, my folks, and my friends are praying for me."

Jehovah Rophe

Then he touched their eyes and said, "According to your faith will it be done to you"; and their sight was restored.
—MATTHEW 9:29–30, NIV

I am the God who heals thee

Since the corner of the upper eyelid had been blown away, a plastic surgeon was called in to give him a skin graft. The next day they wheeled him into surgery and gave him an anesthetic, and he has no recollection of what happened in the operating room after that.

He remembers becoming conscious in his hospital room with both eyes bandaged and with him feeling around on his body to see where they had taken skin for the graft.

"Don't scratch around!" someone commanded firmly, causing him to stop. It was his mother's voice. "They didn't have to operate—a miracle took place," she said. "When they took the bandage off the eyelid preparing for surgery, it was healed over. Praise the Lord."

Daily the nurses changed the bandages, checking mainly to see if the hemorrhaging in his left eye was stopping. Bob could do nothing for himself as he was in total darkness. But on the fifth day, when the nurse changed the bandage on his left eye, he could see the outline of her uniform. The doctor didn't believe it until he removed the bandages and Bob could see his hand.

During the recuperation period the doctor was amazed that Bob didn't want pain medication, but he never filled the prescription because he says he didn't need it. "God took away my pain," he insists. He spent ten days in the hospital, and on the eleventh day after the accident he went to his doctor's office for a complete eye exam.

"This is strange," the doctor said after the exam. "You were blind in this eye, but now you have 20/40 vision. I just can't believe it. But you are never going to see any better than this."

"When the Lord heals you, He doesn't do it three-quarters of the way—He heals you all the way," Bob replied.

Three months later he was back on the set, doing stunts for western movies again.

After a year had passed, he went back to the same eye doctor for a follow-up exam. This time the doctor told him there was no scar on his cornea, the retina was in place, and there was absolutely no sign of hemorrhage. In fact, he had "normal" eyesight! Jesus had indeed healed Bob, and even the doctor had to admit it.

Since his retirement in 1993, Bob and his wife, Lila, travel to teach and preach in churches around the world. Once after he shared his healing story in a California church, a woman began yelling, "I can see! I can see!" She had given up her job as a hairdresser and could no longer drive because of her blindness. But when she heard how the Lord had touched and healed Bob, her faith arose, and she too was healed. Bob says he has encouraged and prayed for a lot of folks with eye damage who have been healed.

He can sympathize with their pain and isolation, but he inspires them to reach out in faith and expect healing from God for themselves.

HELPING THOSE WHO AREN'T HEALED

People are living an average of thirty years longer these days than they did a hundred years ago. At the beginning of the twentieth century, average life expectancy was just over forty-seven years. Now the average is seventy-seven years.[2]

And because we're living longer, many older citizens are afflicted with illnesses that our grandparents never heard of—Alzheimer's being one of them. These patients and their loved ones are finding themselves in a precarious situation as they sort out the differing views regarding recommended treatment.

When former President Ronald Reagan announced publicly that he had Alzheimer's disease, the nation took notice of a malady that affects almost five million Americans. This devastating disorder of the brain's nerve cells impairs memory, thinking, and behavior, robbing the person's personality and eventually leading to death. Most Alzheimer's patients live at home, where almost 75 percent of their care is provided by family and friends.[3]

Caregivers of loved ones with this disease have made such comments as: "I felt like a martyr...I felt abandoned...I felt my world was coming apart at the seams...I tried to negotiate with God, but of course, you can't...I felt anger...I felt intrusion, guilt, loneliness."

Yet others see their role as an opportunity. "This disease slowly robs you of the one you love," one woman said. "But I had to see it as a privilege to care for my husband rather than as a difficult chore." Another asked, "If Mom took care of me in diapers, don't I owe her that now?"

> *Jehovah Rophe*
>
> If you diligently heed the voice of the LORD your God...I will put none of the diseases on you which I have brought on the Egyptians. For I am the LORD who heals you.
>   —EXODUS 15:26
>
> *I am the God who heals thee*

Experts say the sufferers themselves are often convinced they are going crazy or becoming stupid. Because they're unable to talk about their fears and feelings, they act them out in ways that are frightening to family members.

Nell,* a mother who had the sole responsibility of a houseful of children while her husband was stationed in Vietnam, also cared for her mother-in-law for several months when she had Alzheimer's. Finally Nell had to admit her to a nursing home after she

---

* Name changed for privacy

kept running away from home. "It was the hardest thing I ever had to do," she told me (Quin). "The police would find her roaming around and would bring her back, but she was disoriented and didn't want to come into the house."

Now Nell is adjusting to life with her own husband who has been diagnosed with Alzheimer's. Even though he is taking two medications designed to slow down the disease's progression, they plan to move into an assisted living facility near one of their children.

"I've been blessed with a marriage of almost sixty years," Nell said. "My husband still loves to fish and golf and work in the yard. Early on in this disease—often described as teh invisible phase, or silent years, because you have no clue what is wrong—he'd get angry and take off in the car and be gone all day. I'd worry and worry about his safety. Now I've learned to be patient and to not do anything to cause him stress.

"Sometimes I ask him to help me cook so I can give him instructions to follow, and that seems to help his thinking process. Depression was one of his worst symptoms, as well as forgetfulness. I had a long talk with him after the doctor's diagnosis, and we've made some decisions for our future."

We can be grateful that medical advances are being made in providing treatment to help prolong life. But along with treatment, prayer and the loving support of family and friends enhance the patient's quality of life.

A CAREGIVER'S ROLE

Jehovah Rophe

> Have I not commanded you? Be strong and of a good courage; do not be afraid, nor be dismayed, for the LORD your God is with you wherever you go.
>
> —JOSHUA 1:9

I am the God who heals thee

Caregivers are those who help a critically ill patient during his or her time of crisis. While everyone's case is different, many ill patients have some common concerns such as fear of loss of dignity, loss of control, abandonment, or becoming a burden. Others fear dying or suffering pain. As a caregiver you can help by offering hope, encouragement, and comfort. Here are some practical ways:

- Keep the persons company by talking with them, reading the Bible aloud, praying for them, watching movies, or just sitting quietly beside them.

- Encourage them to express their fears and concerns.

- Be willing to listen attentively and let them talk about their life. Try to get them to laugh when appropriate.

- Try not to hide information from patients if they want to be included in discussions about health or future issues concerning them.

- Reassure the patients that you will honor their desires, such as living wills.

- Ask if there is anything you can do, from getting a glass of cold water to writing a letter or making a phone call for them.

- Respect their need for privacy.

QUALITY OF LIFE...
EVEN IN A WHEELCHAIR

When my (Quin's) friend Frances Ewing married Mike, he had already spent five years in a wheelchair, having been paralyzed by polio while serving as a doctor in the U.S. Army. He was a quadriplegic, but he had partial use of one arm.

She used to ask God to give them just ten years of happiness together. They have had forty-eight wonderful years, even though Mike is still confined to a wheelchair. After a stint of rehabilitation and retraining, he began practicing medicine again, this time with severely physically disabled patients. He has taught Bible classes, enjoyed fishing in the Florida gulf as captain of his own houseboat, and traveled with Fran across America driving their motor home.

Yes, he believes in healing. His own son, Mark, was miraculously healed from Hodgkin's disease. Mike has been prayed for many times about his paralysis but hasn't experienced healing in that area. "God's understanding of my innermost being is superior to mine," he said when I asked him about it. "Had I been totally healed, I might not have been as useful to the Lord."

Frances, a nurse, has helped him bounce back from several health challenges. But now he requires almost 24/7 nursing care. In this season of their lives, Fran has learned a new dimension of prayer.

"'Give us this day...' has become my prayer," she said. "I live with a 'today God,' and He is with me in the 'now.' I can't do anything about the future; I can only deal with today—confessing my sins, accepting God's forgiveness, and not living in the past or with regrets. I've learned there is great value in spending my energy on the one day we are given. I have today with Mike—this is our day, and I want to focus on it and make it sweet for him. When it's God's time for him to go, I believe he will just step over into glory, and I would love to be there to put his hand into the hand of Jesus."

Each night Fran prays aloud for the two of them something their friend Corrie ten Boom taught them long ago after she led them to Christ: "Lord, fill our thoughts with You—even our subconscious ones."

When Mike labors to breathe at night, Fran lays her hand on his chest and prays, "Lord Jesus, grant him again the breath of life. May the peace of God invade his body and soul." He will almost immediately start breathing normally. But now she may have to pray that prayer several times during one night. And once in a while she reaches for the oxygen mask.

Her main prayer for him is from Romans 8:18: "Lord Jesus, I know Mike's times are in Your hands. It is You who number his days, but I ask that You give him quality of life all the days of his life. I am very thankful that 'the sufferings of this present time are not worthy to be compared with the glory which shall be revealed in us.'"

Jehovah Rophe

> But David encouraged himself in the LORD his God.
> —1 SAMUEL 30:6, KJV

I am the God who heals thee

Perhaps we should ask ourselves, "Am I prepared to step over into heaven?"

Corrie ten Boom's book has a statement of encouragement:

Think of stepping on shore and finding it heaven, or taking hold of a hand and finding it God's, or breathing new air and finding it celestial, or feeling invigorated and finding it immortality; of passing through a tempest to a new and unknown ground; of waking up well and happy and finding it home.[4]

All of us want to fulfill God's purpose and live out the days He has ordained for us. But are we ready to encourage and comfort others, either for their healing or for their transition into heaven?

You've probably heard about the little boy who told his mother he needed "Jesus with skin on Him" to kiss his hurt knee. We can tell people that Jesus cares about their suffering, but He wants each of us to be "Jesus with skin on Him," so to speak. As we offer them the needed encouragement and spiritual support, we can see them draw closer to the Savior.

Now we'll look further into ways we can help others have their hope restored.

PRAYER

Father God, thank You for sending people of Your choice to pray for us in our darkest hour. Thank You that Jesus endured the agony of the cross—He knew what it was like to suffer and feel pain while facing death. And He did it for me! Thank You, Jesus, for Your selfless sacrifice that opened the way to healing and eternal life. Lord, help me to be sensitive to the pain of others and pray with them with empathy, compassion, and faith. Thank You for giving us power and authority to pray in Your name. Amen.

Christians are people of hope and not despair. Because we know that God, who had the first word, will have the last. He is never thwarted or caught napping by the circumstances of our lives. To have faith in Jesus does not mean we try to pretend that bad things are really good. Rather we know that God will take our difficulties and weave them into purposes we cannot see as yet.[1]

—*Rebecca Manley Pippert*

10

Lord,
RENEW MY HOPE

Yet this I call to mind
   and therefore I have hope:
Because of the LORD's great love we are not consumed,
   for his compassions never fail.
They are new every morning;
   great is your faithfulness....
The LORD is good to those whose hope is in him,
   to the one who seeks him.
               —LAMENTATIONS 3:21–23, 25–26, NIV

HERE IS NOTHING—no situation, illness, or relationship—that cannot be changed by the power of our awesome God. Yet there are secret ingredients: hope and faith. Someone once said, "Hope is putting faith to work when doubting would be easier."

In this chapter you will meet people who maintained their faith and renewed their hope when their circumstances seemed hopeless. Some of them accomplished this through praise and worship, some through dreams and visions, and others through clinging to the promises of Scripture.

Prayer was also a primary component in their healings. As believers we don't sit back and say, "It's up to You, God." He invites us to be persistent in our prayers. As we pray, our desire for the will of God increases, motivating us to press in until our faith and focus are on Him.

Calling the Elders

In biblical times oil was often used in treating the sick—it was considered a type of medicine. But many scholars feel when the apostle James instructed believers to call for church elders to anoint them with oil, it was as an aid to faith. This was an outward "faith statement" that would bring God's response to the prayer for healing.[2]

Oil is often a representation of the Holy Spirit. Some churches regularly have healing services where the church elders anoint the sick with oil while praying for their healing. Others believe if they just call on the Lord in faith that they will receive His touch. Let me (Quin) tell you the story of a friend of mine who read a passage of Scripture and responded to its promise.

Sandy Horn was thirty-four years old when doctors discovered she had five malignant spots—cancer in her neck, in the top and bottom left ribs, in her pelvic bone, and at the tip of her spine. The only remedy the doctor offered for her inoperable cancer was cobalt treatments.

She began to claim the promises of healing, especially as she read and reread these verses from her old King James Bible:

> Is any sick among you? Let him call for the elders of the church; and let them pray over him, anointing him with oil in the name of the Lord: And the prayer of faith shall save the sick, and the Lord shall raise him up.
>
> —James 5:14–15, kjv

Sandy asked God to send her some elders who would pray for her, because she didn't think elders in her own church would consider it appropriate.

She believed she could be healed when no one else did—even her husband, Earl. Over the next few weeks she underwent thirty-four cobalt treatments in the throat area, where the cancer had first shown up. Doctors would later decide which malignant spot was to be treated next.

Late one Sunday night, just before Christmas, her pastor and a visiting Taiwanese missionary knocked on her door. "Could we pray for you?" they asked. Surely these were the elders she had prayed would come.

Her pastor and the missionary prayed specifically that God would heal her. After they left, Sandy stretched out on the bed beside her husband. As she began praising God silently, a strange sensation pulsated through her body, much like an ocean wave engulfing her.

"I felt a surge of power wash up from my toes, extend to my head, and rush back down through my body to my toes again," she said. "I knew the power of Jesus had healed my body! When I told Earl I was healed, he said for me not to get my hopes up."

When Sandy told people she was healed, no one believed her. The first week of February finally rolled around—the time when she was scheduled to go into the hospital for more scans to see where the malignancy was spreading the fastest and where they would give her the next cobalt treatments. But she knew in her heart she would not need them.

After one day of scans and another day of X-rays, the radiologist gave her the results. "Nothing showed up. You have won the first round," he said. Doctors ordered more tests. But again, no sign of cancer. She and Earl asked to see both sets of scans—the original ones showing the five malignant spots and the scans just completed. Looking at them, they knew she was home free. Well! Whole! Healed!

She cried tears of joy. Earl rushed to telephone their closest friends, not afraid now to tell them, "Sandy's been healed by Jesus."

I met Sandy soon after her miracle story and saw all the medical proof records myself. In fact, we became prayer partners, and I still have contact with her. Today, at seventy-two, she lives alone since her husband's death, and she still enjoys good health. Even though the pastors who prayed for her didn't use oil, the Holy Spirit's presence descended on Sandy afterwards as she lay in bed.

"I believed if the elders laid hands on me and prayed, I'd be healed," she said, "Whether they anointed me with oil or not, I was depending on God for healing. I have prayed for others to be healed, and several have been. However, there is no cut-and-dried formula for praying for healing—I just knew I had God's promise of my own healing. I feel I've been living on a miracle for thirty-eight years!"[3]

HOPE PROMPTS ACTION

If ever there was a sick person who refused to give up hope, it was the unnamed woman in the Bible who had hemorrhaged for twelve years. After spending all her money and enduring much at the hands of many physicians, she was no better, but instead was worse. After hearing about Jesus, she said, "If only I may touch His clothes, I shall be made well." When Jesus approached, she pressed through the crowd and reached out for His garment. (See Mark 5:25–34.)

It didn't matter that she was unclean. She was desperate and determined. And as soon as she was able to touch His robe, her blood flow was dried up, and she felt the manifestation of healing in her body.

Her contact got Jesus' attention as He felt power go out of Him. This was not just the jostling of the crowd; this was a touch of faith. When He asked who in that huge crowd had touched Him, she fell down before Him and admitted the truth. Instead of scolding, He spoke hope to her! "Daughter, your faith has made you well. Go in peace, and be healed of your affliction" (v. 34).

Now hope does not disappoint, because the love of God has been poured out in our hearts by the Holy Spirit who was given to us.

—ROMANS 5:5

What an inspiration her action is to us. Sometimes we have to get past what other people may think or say and just do whatever it takes to get to Jesus. Undaunted, we have to hang on to hope!

A doctor who believes in the power of hope writes:

The greatest danger...is that a patient will become passive, give up, or fail to resist and fight against the sickness or disease.

...A feisty patient awakens, stirs up, and undergirds his natural will to live through faith in God, trust in His Word, and ready cooperation with what he must do in the natural....He does not sit back and accept what is happening to his body, but focuses his attention and energy on the manifestation of healing.

...This means that at times we must have a "lively aggressiveness" in claiming and taking possession of the promises that are ours as children of God.[4]

Various Methods of Healing

Nancy Gibes-Curry, a nurse, told me (Quin) that healing is "one of God's holy mysteries" to her. Dramatic healing has not come every time she's prayed for healing. But on occasion she has seen or experienced firsthand God's supernatural healing power—at small home prayer groups, at large healing crusades, and while watching Christian television. While attending Charismatic meetings in the 1970s, she began to believe that Jesus was still healing today, despite the fact her church taught that signs and wonders had ceased. She shares some of her healing experiences:

- "I had endured sinus allergies for ten years. I usually slept with my mouth open all night, and in the morning my tongue felt like a piece of cardboard. One night at a home prayer meeting I finally asked for prayers. Friends laid hands on me, and one prayed, 'Lord, we lift up Nancy's nose to you for healing.' We chuckled at the simplicity of the prayer, but we were combining our faith, and I knew I was healed after prayer. Sure enough, I had no more suffering from sneezing, itching eyes or stuffiness in my nose. God used our faith!"

- "In the 1980s I began to experience pain in my joints, especially in my left hip, elbows, and all fingers. I liked to make homemade bread but had to stop, as I could not knead it anymore. Starting the car with the key finger was so painful, and getting out of the car on that left hip was rough. I tried the health food route for six weeks with no improvement whatever. I changed doctors, as I had no diagnosis or treatment. A blood tier showed rheumatoid arthritis in the beginning stages. I was told to take aspirin several times daily for inflammation, but it gave me diarrhea. One evening at the Bible study we attended, the teacher said he felt God was going to heal folks who came up for laying on of hands. I knew it was for me! I got in line and received prayer. Nothing happened as far as I could tell. But the next morning all my pain was gone and never returned. I told anyone who would listen! Again, I felt a sense of being loved and special to God."

- "I had been diagnosed with cervical polyps and was going to have them removed surgically. At a small meeting the group prayed over those needing healing with the laying on of hands. When they prayed for me, I felt something like electricity go through my body. I couldn't wait for the doctor to confirm I was healed. Sure enough, the next week during my exam the doctor could find no polyps. On the way home I found a seat in a quiet church and just sat there basking in God's love."

- "I had a hysterectomy in 1984, but while at the hospital I picked up a staph infection. The potent antibiotic they gave me caused severe diarrhea in addition to the fever, malaise, and postoperative pain. One day I was so sick I just lay on the couch, but I turned on a Christian television program. While watching *The 700 Club*, the show's host suddenly had a word of knowledge that a woman with female problems was being healed. I said, 'That's me!' From that moment on I began to recover, even without taking the antibiotic. God knew me and my sickness, and He touched me through a stranger on TV!"

- "My husband, Wayne, had injured his left knee while playing high school football. The X-ray showed no broken bones, but torn blood vessels left his knee black and blue up into the thigh area. Over the years as it ached and became very painful, he wore an elastic brace while racing motorcycles or playing volleyball. Doctors recommended

surgery, but he kept postponing it. One night we went
to a big Charismatic crusade just for the fellowship and
anointed preaching, but at the end the healing evangelist
invited people to get in line for healing prayer. Wayne went
up front, behind about twenty other people. As prayer was
offered for others, the atmosphere in the room seemed
charged with God's presence. Wayne suddenly felt something like warm water running down his shin from his
knee. To his amazement, he had an instant healing before
the evangelist could even lay hands on him. God healed
him supernaturally right where he stood, and the pain
never returned."

These are just a few of the miracles Nancy shared. No doubt
you, like Nancy, have experienced God's touch at times when you
least expected it. The point is, there are no formulas for healing,
and we must not limit God by believing we can receive through
only one method.

BELIEVING GOD FOR A FAMILY

We firmly believe there is no situation that is beyond God's intervention. That includes infertility. Jim and Michal Ann Goll are the
parents of four beautiful children—most of them adults now. But
as a barren couple, there was a time when they wondered if they
would ever become parents.

They had been married for several years, pastoring a small
church in Missouri, and longed for a family. One night Jim had
a short dream in which the Holy Spirit told him he'd have a son,
and his name would be Justin. He and Michal Ann got excited. As
the months passed with no outward sign of pregnancy, they realized God didn't tell them *how* they would have their son. Could He
have meant adoption?

They applied to an adoption agency, but before completing the process, they both felt strongly that this was not God's plan for them. They continued trusting, not just in a dream but in the God of the dream. A year passed, and they were still childless.

After Michal Ann underwent more medical tests and a laparoscopy, the doctor told them it was impossible for her to have children. Her uterine cavity was five to six times the normal size, and the lining was not viable enough to sustain life.

Now that they had the hard facts, they turned the diagnosis into this persistent prayer: "God, You gave us Your holy Word. You gave us a dream. We have believing people of prayer agreeing with us. We cannot perform this thing ourselves. We are totally dependent on You to bring it to pass. Fulfill the dream You gave us. Give us a miracle in the great name of Jesus."

They pronounced healing scriptures with declarations of faith and commanded life to come over their bodies. Still they saw no change.

Michal Ann remembers those cloudy days vividly, "We depleted every option we could think of in our search for an answer to our complex circumstances," she said. "Most of all, we prayed. We then rebuked our barrenness and declared God's Word over our bodies. We did everything we knew to do physically, medically, and spiritually. Yet, in spite of all of this, after six years, all attempts ended up in the same place—with no fruit. Let me tell you, it was incredibly painful."

Some time later, when a healing evangelist visited their church, Jim grabbed Michal Ann and went up to the platform to receive prayer. The evangelist was quiet for a time; then he said to Michal Ann, "Oh, I see you as a joyful mother of three children."

Jehovah Rophe

> Forever, O LORD,
> Your word is settled in heaven.
> Your faithfulness endures to all generations;
> You established the earth, and it abides.
> —PSALM 119:89–90

I am the God who heals thee

Jim describes what happened next. "The power of the Holy Spirit came on us, and at the same moment we fell like timber to the floor. The presence of the Lord Jesus was so strong and tangibly powerful that we were unable to stand to our feet. Or perhaps we dropped to the floor out of shock. We had been trying to believe God for one child. Now [he] said he saw three."

Soon after the first of the year Michal Ann caught the flu, but no amount of prayer seemed to help, so Jim took her to the doctor. After the examination the doctor tried to look straight-faced as he delivered the news. "This is the kind of sickness that's not going to leave for a long time. You're going to have a baby."

They were elated, shocked, and thrilled. On October 4, 1983, Justin Wayne Goll was born, followed by Grace Ann, Tyler, and finally Rachel, who was a real surprise! The Lord had spoken to Michal Ann's heart that she must fight for her children. Jim says the children came as a result of prayer, fighting the enemy, and supernatural acts of God's power.

What about the healing evangelist who had prophesied three children? He answered by saying with a grin, "In the prophetic you see in part and you prophesy in part. I was seeing only three-fourths of the part!"

Jim says anywhere along the way they could have given up, but by God's grace they continued to believe their dream, even when obstacles loomed before their faces. He believes God wants to heal other barren women just as He healed his wife.[5]

Whether our problem is cancer, arthritis, infertility, tuberculosis, or any other malady, we can call upon the Lord to release His healing power to us. In the next story, the faith and courage of a child led to a dramatic healing that challenged both the doctors and the court.

A VISION OF JESUS

Katherine Ellis was only ten and a half when she was diagnosed with T-cell lymphoma in November 2000. In just three weeks she had lost considerable weight, and lymph nodes the size of walnuts were protruding all over her body, especially in her neck. One lymph node was a mass extending across her chest—even covering her heart.

To keep her veins from breaking down, doctors inserted a portacath in her chest so chemotherapy treatments could be administered into the main artery in her chest. But after receiving chemotherapy and other drugs for three months to fight her disease, Katherine was experiencing severe side effects, including seizures and the inability to straighten her body to an upright position. Since her parents were in ministry, they contacted many pastors and friends both in the United States and overseas, asking them to pray and fast for her complete healing.

One night when she was home from the hospital, her mother, Phyllis, went to check to be sure that her daughter wasn't having a seizure. She found Katherine weeping. "What's wrong?" she asked.

Katherine explained she'd had a vision of Jesus—she had seen His face on the ceiling above her bed. His head was dripping in oil.

He had said, "Katherine, you are healed of your disease."

She begged her mom not to make her take any more chemo. At her next doctor's visit, Phyllis asked for tests to check her progress. After the laboratory analysis was completed, the doctor reported her blood work was normal, including her white blood cell count. Her spleen was no longer protruding in her abdomen. Everything was back in place, and the mass across her chest was completely gone. Doctors couldn't believe there had been such a complete change in her body. She had no sign of cancer.

"We asked the doctors to stop the chemo treatments, but to have Katherine keep her regular appointments so they could observe her or test her," Phyllis explained. "But it wasn't normal to stop the treatments after only three months, so we found ourselves in court, with the hospital insisting she stay in treatment."

Katherine's parents realized that if they lost in court, their child could be taken from their custody, removed from their home, and forced to continue chemotherapy. But instead of hiring a lawyer to represent them, they simply trusted the Lord. They said they were asking to stop her treatments because Katherine's body was radically changed, not because of "religious beliefs." There was no proof that she had cancer.

During the final court session, after Katherine's doctors had testified before the judge, Phyllis was allowed to question the doctor.

"Did you not say to me that Katherine had reached a point where you no longer knew how to treat her?" Phyllis asked.

"Yes," the doctor answered.

"Didn't I tell you that you could observe her over the next few months during her regular appointment times?"

"Yes," she said.

"Well, if that is what she asked you to do—then do it," the judge ordered the doctors.

Katherine was allowed to go home with her parents and did not have to have another treatment! For a while she went back to the doctor every three months for a checkup, then every six months. Now she only goes in once a year. She was so glad when her hair grew back in and she had no more side effects from medications.

Before the cancer ordeal Phyllis wasn't sure whether her daughter had experienced salvation. She had prayed, "Lord, prove that You are the God of Katherine, not the God of her mommy or daddy." After having a vision of the Lord in her room and being completely healed, Katherine's life was dramatically changed.

At the time of this writing, she is sixteen, and her mom homeschools her along with her two younger sisters. Katherine hopes to go to college to study music, majoring in voice, and to someday have a ministry in child evangelism. There is still no sign that she ever had cancer.

He is the God of yesterday, today, and tomorrow. The God who heals us!

FINDING HOPE DESPITE HIV DIAGNOSIS

At the 2005 Aglow International Conference in Nashville, with 106 nations represented, I (Quin) heard the amazing healing testimony of Segametsi Mothibatsela, an attorney from Southern Africa. I followed up to get more details about her adventure in faith to share with you. Here is Segametsi's story in her own words.

———◆◆◆———

In 1998 I discovered that I was HIV positive. As a brand-new Christian and not yet very knowledgeable about God and His ways, the sense of loss, panic, shock, shame, and absolute terror I felt at the discovery was overwhelming.

I was living alone on the Caribbean island of Dominica for a work assignment there at the time. Lying in bed at night, I would sweat profusely from fear, believing that each night could be my last. I wondered what would happen to my children, who were ten and fifteen years of age at the time. I didn't want them to grow up without a mother.

Jehovah Rophe

> Fear not, for I am with you;
> Be not dismayed, for I am your God.
> I will strengthen you,
> Yes, I will help you,
> I will uphold you with My righteous right hand.
>
> —ISAIAH 41:10

I am the God who heals thee

In the five years preceding my move to the Caribbean, my life had been traumatized by heavy indebtedness, a painful divorce, disinterest in my job, and an attempted suicide. Surely neither my children nor I could take any more tragedy in our lives. I felt I couldn't talk about my condition to anyone—not even the doctor who confirmed the diagnosis.

But I was to discover that the God who had divinely taken me from my country, Botswana, in Southern Africa to a faraway land would reveal Himself to me in a mighty way. Shortly before taking the assignment in Dominica, I remarried and became a Christian. From the moment I was saved, God gave me a great love for His Word. Day and night, I would devour the Word and weep as I saw myself, as through a mirror. For much of my life I had been walking contrary to God's ways.

I had two law degrees, a successful career in Dominica, a beautiful home, and good health. Now, when I faced certain death, none of this seemed to matter anymore. I'd heard about recently discovered drugs for HIV, yet I knew they would only buy time; they could not cure me. I had children to look after, and I wanted to live. But that would take a miracle.

As I read the many promises of total forgiveness and healing I found in God's Word, one verse especially convinced me that if anyone could change my situation, it was God. The verse says, "God is not a man, that He should lie; nor a son of man, that He should repent" (Num. 23:19).

He was not asking me for money or anything else—just asking that I should believe Him. Since I had nothing to lose, I decided to trust Him for the impossible.

One day during my prayer time, the Lord told me to read the first chapter of Genesis—that my answer was there. I read that in the beginning God spoke to the chaos in the world. The Holy Spirit revealed to me that if I would speak God's Word, and not mine, into the chaos in my life, I would see the chaos transformed to victory. For every situation God's Word has a promise, so I began searching the scriptures on healing and speaking them over my life.

As I read story after story of God's extraordinary healing power, I became more and more convinced that I would be healed. I determined that no matter how long it took, I would hang in there until my healing manifested. When I read in Mark 11:25–26 about the necessity of forgiving others, I made a list of the people with whom I had taken offense. I told the Lord I forgave them, and I did. I confessed to God that I was to blame for my state because I had not lived according to His Word, and I asked Him to forgive me and cleanse me.

But the more I prayed, the sicker I became, the thinner I became, and the more questions those around me began to ask about what was wrong. I just told them I was exercising too much and refused to be discouraged.

Then I began to speak to my body. I commanded the pain in my bones and chest to leave, and I told my lungs that they would never suffer from tuberculosis or pneumonia. I told my head to stop aching and that my brain would never contract meningitis because, according to Psalm 139:14, I was fearfully and wonderfully made by God. I declared that my body was the temple of the Holy Spirit and should not accommodate the HIV virus, and I commanded it to leave. I did this every single day.

When I left the Caribbean and returned to my home in Botswana, I was faced with the task of breaking the news to my husband. It was a terrifying thought, but I prayed fervently for God's favor and help and asked Him to prepare my husband's heart. I told him and assured him that if he wanted to divorce me, I would understand. He was silent for some time, then said he would not divorce me, but he would pray with me for God to heal me. I was as stunned as I was relieved, and since that time I've not ceased to thank God for my husband and ask that he should never be sick. God answered that prayer, because my husband did not contract the virus.

Four years after my diagnosis, I began hearing testimonies of how the Lord was healing thousands of HIV-positive people in Uganda, so my husband and I went there for a conference. My faith soared to new heights as I heard one healing testimony after another. But when one of the ministers who had been healed of HIV called for those who had the virus to come forward for prayer, I could not get out of my chair. I was just too ashamed and too afraid. Afterwards I tried to see the minister to have her pray for me in private, but I never got the opportunity.

For weeks after returning home I could not pray. The fear and desperation returned, and I lost interest in life. One day I came across Psalm 118:17: "I shall not die, but live, and declare the works of the LORD." It was as though God had spoken the words directly to me. I began once more to pray with fervor and to believe that God would heal me. Sometimes I just thanked God in advance for my healing and praised Him for who He is.

At the end of that year, the minister I had met in Uganda visited

Botswana, and I again went to her meeting. Again, she made an altar call for those who were sick with the HIV/AIDS virus. "You should not be ashamed, because once the enemy is exposed, he no longer has power over you," she said.

I decided that that night, no matter who said what, I would receive my healing. I was the first person at the altar. You could have heard a pin drop. Everyone was so shocked. *I* had the virus? *A lawyer?* But I didn't care. All I knew was that I did not want to die and that I had God's promises of life.

When the minister laid hands on me I felt the power of God go through my body, and I *knew* that I was healed. I couldn't sleep that night. In my spirit, I kept hearing, *Read Psalm 30.* When I read these verses I began to scream and shout, then did a jig in my room:

> O LORD my God, I cried out to You, and You have healed me. O LORD, You have brought my soul up from the grave; You have kept me alive, that I should not go down to the pit.... You have turned for me my mourning into dancing; You have put off my sackcloth and clothed me with gladness, to the end that my glory may sing praise to You and not be silent. O LORD my God, I will give thanks to You forever.
> —PSALM 30:2–3, 11–12

When I woke up the following morning, all the pain was gone from my body. My head was clear. I felt more alert and alive than I had for a long time. The grass looked greener—everything looked *so* beautiful. I'd been sick for so long that I'd forgotten what it was to be well. It felt wonderful.

My husband and I went to have our blood tested for the virus. As the technician took the blood sample from me, I was busy praying in tongues. HIV *negative* was the report that came back for both of us! I left the testing center rejoicing and praising God, and I immediately began to testify about my healing.

Some people believed that indeed God had healed me. Others

were cynical and mocked. Others were polite and disinterested and said "how nice" or "how interesting" it was. I told them, and continue to declare across the world, that it is neither "nice" nor "interesting." It is powerful, extraordinary, amazing, and totally mind-boggling!

Jehovah Rophe

But as for me, I will always have hope; I will praise you more and more. My mouth will tell of your righteousness, of your salvation all day long.

—Psalm 71:14–15, niv

I am the God who heals thee

Several doctors in my country told me I was misleading people and that I should shut my mouth. I told them I would never remain silent—and indeed I never shall. I have been healed and have continued to enjoy God's goodness. I have never felt better in my life. God has used my testimony to bring hope, encouragement, and even healing to many as I have shared it.

God is able to step in and do the impossible if you let Him. His Word works! All you need to do is apply it and believe, and watch God amaze you.*

———————

We received confirmation of the above testimony quite unexpectedly. In e-mail correspondence with a missionary friend living in Botswana, I (Ruthanne) mentioned that Quin and I had a great story for our new book of a woman in her country being healed after being diagnosed with HIV. My friend wrote back to say she's well acquainted with Segametsi (she calls her "Miggy") and her

———

* To contact Segametsi, write to: Segametsi Mothibatsela, P. O. Box 81412, Gaborone, Botswana, Southern Africa.

miraculous testimony. The two serve together on the national board for Aglow in Botswana.

HE IS STILL THE GREAT PHYSICIAN

We come back to the premise we established at the beginning of this book: a health crisis gives us an opportunity to reach a deeper understanding that the same God who created our body also has the power to heal it.

A good example of this was the popular minister Dr. A. B. Simpson (1843–1902). When he was in his late thirties, a doctor told him that because of his poor health he wouldn't live to be forty. Dr. Simpson couldn't even walk without agonizing pain. In desperation, he searched his Bible and became convinced that healing was part of Christ's atonement. How he longed for this experience himself!

So he prayed, asking the Lord to meet the needs of his body until his work on earth was finished. As he prayed, every fiber in his body tingled with the sense of the Lord's presence. Over the next three years the proof of his healing became evident. In that space of time, he preached more than a thousand sermons and sometimes conducted as many as twenty meetings in one week.

He lived to be seventy-six and, according to one biographer, became "one of the greatest exponents of divine healing that the church had seen in a thousand years." His strong stand on healing upset some of his denominational colleagues, but he didn't allow that to dampen his zeal for what he called the fourfold gospel: Christ as Savior, Sanctifier, Healer, and the coming King.

Dr. Simpson started the Christian and Missionary Alliance, established a publishing house, founded a college, and wrote scores of books. Today, more than a hundred years after his death, his printed sermons still reach multitudes of people for Christ.[6]

Another example that Jesus is still the Great Physician is our ninety-two-year-old friend Freda Lindsay, cofounder of Christ For The Nations in Dallas. When she was still a young bride, she was diagnosed with tuberculosis in both lungs and told to remain in bed for at least a year. This was long before any medical solutions for TB had been developed, so bedrest was about the only treatment.

But her husband Gordon was an evangelist who strongly believed in healing. He talked to her about what the Bible teaches on healing and encouraged her to trust God to intervene. Freda went to her room to pray and ask God to forgive her of every sin of omission or commission she could think of before having Gordon pray for her.

"After communing with the Lord for several hours, I felt completely clean within," she wrote. "I knew I was ready to be healed!"

That evening she and Gordon prayed together, then he began to rebuke the enemy and ask God to heal his wife in Jesus' name. Freda declared that she was healed and began walking back and forth in the room praising God and thanking Him, even though she didn't "feel" healed. She continued praising God, rested for a few minutes, then began walking and praising again. In less than two weeks she left with her husband on an evangelistic trip, and the two continued with a healing and teaching ministry for several decades. To this day Freda is a gold mine of information about the healing movement of the twentieth century.[7]

The Lindsays also established Christ For The Nations Institute (CFNI) in Dallas, Texas, where thousands have studied the Word of God and learned that miracles have not ceased. With "Mom Lindsay's" encouragement, many of these students have gone around the world with the full gospel message.

Both of us (Ruthanne and Quin) had the privilege of knowing

this remarkable woman when we lived on the campus at CFNI. Sometimes we walked the jogging track there with her and were continually amazed by her stamina and her sharp mind. I (Ruthanne) worked for a few years on her editorial staff, while my husband, John, was an instructor at the Institute for twenty-three years.

As Freda Lindsay and others you have met in these pages discovered, Jesus is still the Great Physician who is "touched with the feeling of our infirmities" (Heb. 4:15, kjv).

We hope that as you have read this book you've come to know God more intimately by one of His names: *Jehovah Rophe,* "the Lord who heals, restores, or makes whole." This word *Rophe* refers to a God who heals the entire person, not just the body. What a compassionate, all-encompassing heavenly Father we have!

We conclude by praying this scripture for you:

> Now may the God of hope fill you with all joy and peace in believing, that you may abound in hope by the power of the Holy Spirit.
>
> —Romans 15:13

PRAYER

Faithful God, I thank You that You never change...that Your mercies are new every morning. Help me to trust You with my health, my future, and my life. Help me to stay focused on You and Your promises, because You alone are my rock and my hope. I worship You in Jesus' name. Amen.

Epilogue

$\mathcal{M}$Y FRIEND Beth Alves, whose home is only a few miles from mine in the Texas Hill Country, was in town recently and phoned to catch up on news. Because of her ministry travel schedule, we seldom see each other. I noticed she was struggling to get her breath as she talked. When I mentioned it, she said she had a call in to her doctor, as she'd been having the problem for several days.

A few hours later I returned from running errands and had a voice mail message asking me to pray for Beth. One of her staff members had taken her to the hospital, where they were running tests. The next day I got word that the cardiologist had told her, "You've had a significant heart attack, but we don't know yet the extent of the damage until we do a heart catheterization procedure."

I immediately called Quin to ask her to pray and to send out a request to her circle of prayer partners.

Word went out by phone and e-mail to people all over the world to pray for Beth. After years of her worldwide travel, teaching, and inspiring others to pray, now it was time for us to seriously pray for her. I had to go out of town on a teaching trip, but I kept calling Beth's office to get the doctor's report. Finally I got a voice mail message that no surgery was necessary.

More than a week later I was able to talk to Beth and get the full story. She said that before they anesthetized her, she had to sign permission forms for several possible solutions in case they were needed. Based on what the procedure would show about her heart, the surgeon expected either to put in a stent, do a balloon procedure to open blocked arteries, replace a valve, install a pacemaker, or possibly do full open-heart surgery.

But none of those procedures proved to be necessary.

"He said the upper third of my heart had suffered damage, but he was amazed that all my arteries were clean," Beth told me. "He said he could see where the blockages had been, but it 'looked like something had gone in there and blown them out.' Those were his exact words."

"Wow! That says something about the power of prayer," I responded.

"I believe that was the wind of the Holy Spirit!" Beth continued. "The doctor said he felt the damage that was done could be treated through medication. I'm believing God for full restoration."

I thought about the decades-long journey of faith Beth has been on since she first discovered the scripture about laying hands on the sick (Mark 16:17–18) and prayed for her daughter to be healed of an inoperable brain tumor. (See her story in chapter two.)

Of course she has experienced other answers to prayer for healing over the years, but none as dramatic as this with her heart. How fitting that we can share her testimony as an epilogue for our book on healing.

Quin and I believe that where there's life, there's always hope for healing and restoration. Be assured that prayer definitely makes a difference!

—Ruthanne Garlock
June 2, 2006

Notes

CHAPTER 1
LORD, I NEED YOUR HELP

1. Jack W. Hayford, *Hayford's Bible Handbook* (Nashville, TN: Thomas Nelson, 1995), 30.
2. *New Spirit-Filled Life Bible*, Jack W. Hayford, editor (Nashville, TN: Thomas Nelson, 1991), 936.
3. Adapted from Quin Sherrer, *Miracles Happen When You Pray* (Grand Rapids, MI: Zondervan, 1997), 118–119 (book is now out of print); recent interviews; and data from http://www.wildpharm .com.
4. James Strong, *Strong's Exhaustive Concordance of the Bible* (updated) (N.p.: Riverside World, 1996), s.v. *qara'*, OT:7121, "call."
5. Ibid., s.v. *hagah*, OT:1897, "meditate."

CHAPTER 2
LORD, INCREASE MY FAITH

1. Charles S. Price, *The Real Faith* (Plainfield, NJ: Logos International, 1972), 33.
2. Stanley Howard Frodsham, *Smith Wigglesworth, Apostle of Faith* (Springfield, MO: Gospel Publishing House, 1948, 2002), 111.
3. Graham Cooke, *The Language of Promise* (Kent, England: Sovereign World, Ltd., 2004), 53–54.
4. Strong, *Strong's Exhaustive Concordance of the Bible* (updated), s.v. *sozo*, NT:4982, "save."
5. *New Spirit-Filled Life Bible*, 1402.

CHAPTER 3
LORD, IT HURTS

1. Smith Wigglesworth, *The Anointing of His Spirit*, Wayne Warner, editor (Ann Arbor, MI: Servant, 1994), 113.
2. Joy Dawson, *Some of the Ways of God in Healing* (Seattle, WA: YWAM Publishing, 1991), 29–31.
3. Dr. Paul Brand and Philip Yancey, *In His Image* (Grand Rapids, MI: Zondervan, 1984), 286–287.
4. "Kingdom Dynamics," *New Spirit-Filled Life Bible*, 1624–1625.
5. Adapted from Quin Sherrer and Ruthanne Garlock, *A Woman's Guide to Getting Through Tough Times* (Ann Arbor, MI: Servant, 1998), 192–193 (book is now out of print); and recent interviews.
6. Ibid., 148–149; and recent interviews.
7. Brand and Yancey, *In His Image*, 291.

CHAPTER 4
LORD, I NEED PEACE

1. Stuart and Brenda Blanch, *Learning of God: Readings From Amy Carmichael* (Fort Washington, PA: CLC, 1985), 129.
2. Hilary E. MacGregor, "Prayer's Aid to the Ill Still Being Assessed," *Los Angeles Times*, reprinted in the *Dallas Morning News*, July 16, 2005, G-1.
3. Strong, *Strong's Exhaustive Concordance of the Bible* (updated), s.v. *sumphoneo*, NT:485, "agree."
4. Dr. Kenneth J. Bakken, *Journey Into God* (Minneapolis, MN: Augsburg Fortress, 2000), 87.
5. Adapted from Sherrer, *Miracles Happen When You Pray*, 121–144; and recent interview.
6. Chuck Pierce, "Understanding and Breaking the Cycle of Infirmity" *Global Prayer News*, Colorado Springs, CO, Vol. 6, No. 3, July–September 2005, 6, 11.

CHAPTER 5
LORD, I NEED PERSPECTIVE

1. F. F. Bosworth, *Christ the Healer* (Grand Rapids, MI: Revell, 1973, 2000), 21.

2. Adapted from Quin Sherrer and Ruthanne Garlock, *A Woman's Guide to Breaking Bondages* (Ann Arbor, MI: Servant, 1994), 182–183 (book is now out of print).

3. Che Ahn, *How to Pray for Healing* (Ventura, CA: Regal, 2004), 104–105.

4. Judson Cornwall, *Praying the Scriptures* (Lake Mary, FL: Charisma House, 1988), 109–110.

5. Adapted from Sherrer, *Miracles Happen When You Pray*, 62–64; and recent interview.

6. Wilford Reidt, *John G. Lake, a Man Without Compromise* (Tulsa, OK: Harrison House, 1989), 70.

7. International Association of Healing Rooms, http://www .healingrooms.com (accessed June 22, 2006).

8. Francis MacNutt, O.P., *The Power to Heal* (Notre Dame, IN: Ave Maria Press, 1977), 39.

9. Ibid., 57–61.

10. Dutch Sheets, *Intercessory Prayer* (Ventura, CA: Regal Books, 1996), 103–105, and from Quin's personal notes taken while Pastor Sheets preached.

11. Reidt, *John G. Lake, a Man Without Compromise*, 56.

CHAPTER 6
LORD, HELP ME MAKE RIGHT DECISIONS

1. Reginald Cherry, MD, *Healing Prayer* (Nashville, TN: Thomas Nelson, 1999), 116–117.

2. James Goll, http://www.encountersnetwork.com (accessed January 5, 2005).

3. Ibid.

4. Adapted from Gordon Lindsay, *Prayer That Moves Mountains* (Dallas, TX: Christ For The Nations Publications, 1959, 1973), 120. Originally adapted from Grace Perkins Ousler, "A Question of Courage," *Reader's Digest School Reader*, 1959, condensed and adapted from a *Guideposts* article.

5. *New Spirit-Filled Life Bible*, 264.

6. Jordan S. Rubin, *The Maker's Diet* (Lake Mary, FL: Siloam, 2004), 3.

7. Elizabeth Frazao of the U.S. Department of Agriculture, reported by Dr. Don Colbert, in "The Great Exchange," *Enjoying Life Everyday*, March 2005, 18.

8. Rubin, *The Maker's Diet*, 82.

9. *Matthew Henry's Commentary on the Whole Bible*, New Modern Edition, Electronic Database. Copyright © 1991, Hendrickson Publishers, Inc.

CHAPTER 7
LORD, RESTORE MY JOY

1. E. Stanley Jones, *Christian Maturity* (Nashville, TN: Abingdon Press, 1957), reprinted in *God's Treasury of Virtues* (Tulsa, OK: Honor Books, 1995), 77.

2. Dutch Sheets, *Tell Your Heart to Beat Again* (Ventura, CA: Regal, 2002), 76.

3. National Institute of Mental Health, "Bipolar Disorder," Melissa Spearing, NIH Publication No. 3679, updated 5/09/2006, http://www.nimh.nih.gov/Publicat/bipolar.cfm#sup1 (accessed May 25, 2006).

4. Ibid.

5. Don Colbert, MD, *What You Don't Know May Be Killing You!* (Lake Mary, FL: Siloam, 2000, 2004), 92.

6. William Speed Weed, "I Am Moe's Funny Bone—How Laughter Affects Every Part of Your Body," *Reader's Digest*, September 2005, 96–97.

7. Strong, *Strong's Exhaustive Concordance of the Bible* (updated), s.v. *giyl*, OT:1523.

8. *New Spirit-Filled Life Bible*, 946.

9. Ruth Myers, *31 Days of Praise* (Sisters, OR: Multnomah Books, 1994), 127.

CHAPTER 8
LORD, RESTORE MY RELATIONSHIPS

1. James Robison, "The Holy Spirit and Restoration," *New Spirit-Filled Life Bible*, 1859.

2. *Vine's Expository Dictionary of Biblical Words* (Nashville, TN: Thomas Nelson Publishers, 1985), used in PC Study Bible software, copyright © 2000.

3. *Spirit-Filled Life Bible*, study notes, 1780.

4. Judson Cornwall, *Dying With Grace* (Lake Mary, FL: Charisma House, 2004), 75–76.

CHAPTER 9
LORD, MAKE ME AN ENCOURAGER

1. Traci Mullins and Ann Spangler, *Vitamins for Your Soul* (New York: Doubleday, 1997), 81.

2. National Vital Statistics Reports, "Data Highlights—Life Expectancy," National Center for Health Statistics, http://www.cdc.gov/nchs/fastats/lifexpec.htm (accessed June 23, 2006).

3. Alzheimer's Association, http://www.alz.org/Resources (accessed August 6, 2005).

4. Corrie ten Boom, *He Cares, He Comforts, in Sickness and in Health* (Old Tappan, NJ: Fleming H. Revell, 1977), 92.

CHAPTER 10
LORD, RENEW MY HOPE

1. Rebecca Manley Pippert, *Hope Has Its Reasons* (New York: Harper & Row, 1989), 203–204.

2. *The NIV Study Bible*, Kenneth Barker, general editor (Grand Rapids, MI: Zondervan, 1985), 1885.

3. Adapted from Sherrer, *Miracles Happen When You Pray*, 126–130, and recent interviews.

4. Cherry, *Healing Prayer*, 113.

5. Adapted from Jim W. Goll, *Kneeling on the Promises* (Grand Rapids, MI: Chosen Books, 1999), 40–49, and from personal interviews.

6. Adapted from Catherine Marshall, "Timeless Treasures," *SpiritLed Woman*, February/March 2002, 66–67; also, notes by Charles W. Nienkirchen and A. W. Tozer, as posted November 10, 2005, http://churchinwestland.org.

7. Mrs. Gordon Lindsay, *My Diary Secrets* (Dallas, TX: Christ For The Nations, 1976, 1982), 51–54.

Recommended Reading

Ahn, Che. *How to Pray for Healing*. Ventura, CA: Regal Books, 2004.

Alcorn, Randy. *Heaven*. Carol Stream, IL: Tyndale House, 2004.

Anderson, Neil T., and Hal Baumchen. *Finding Hope Again*. Ventura, CA: Regal Books, 1999.

Bosworth, F. F. *Christ the Healer*. Grand Rapids, MI: Revell, a division of Baker Book House, 1973, 2000.

Cherry, Reginald, MD. *Bible Health Secrets*. Lake Mary, FL: Siloam, 2003.

———. *Healing Prayer*. Nashville, TN: Thomas Nelson Publishers, 1999.

Colbert, Don, MD. *What You Don't Know May Be Killing You!* Lake Mary, FL: Siloam, 2000, 2004.

Cornwall, Judson. *Dying With Grace*. Lake Mary, FL: Charisma House, 2004.

———. *Praying the Scriptures*. Lake Mary, FL: Charisma House, 1988, 1997.

Dawson, Joy. *Some of the Ways of God in Healing*. Seattle, WA: YWAM Publishing, 1991.

Garlock, H. B., with Ruthanne Garlock. *Before We Kill and Eat You*. Ventura, CA: Regal Books, 2003.

Goll, Jim W. *Kneeling on the Promises*. Grand Rapids, MI: Chosen Books, 1999.

Lindsay, Mrs. Gordon. *My Diary Secrets*. Dallas, TX: Christ For The Nations, 1976, 1982.

MacNutt, Francis. *The Power to Heal*. Notre Dame, IN: Ave Maria Press, 1977.

Marshall, Catherine. *Light In My Darkest Night*. New York: Hearst Corp, through arrangement with Chosen Books, 1989.

Reidt, Wilford. *John G. Lake, a Man Without Compromise*. Tulsa, OK: Harrison House, 1989.

Rubin, Jordan S. *The Maker's Diet*. Lake Mary, FL: Siloam, 2004, 2005.

Sheets, Dutch. *Hope Restored*. Ventura, CA: Regal Books, 2004.

———. *Intercessory Prayer*. Ventura, CA: Regal Books, 1996.

Sherrer, Quin, and Ruthanne Garlock. *A Beginner's Guide to Receiving the Holy Spirit*. Ventura, CA: Regal Books, 2002.

———. *A Woman's Guide to Spiritual Warfare*. Ventura, CA: Regal Books, 1990.

———. *The Spiritual Warrior's Prayer Guide*. Ventura, CA: Regal Books, 1992.

Simpson, A. B. *The Best of A. B. Simpson*. Camp Hill, PA: Christian Publications, 1987.

Spangler, Ann. *A Miracle a Day*. Grand Rapids, MI: Zondervan, 1996.

———. *An Angel a Day*. Grand Rapids, MI: Zondervan, 1994.

Stormont, George. *Wigglesworth: A Man Who Walked With God*. Tulsa, OK: Harrison House, 1981.

Wigglesworth, Smith. *Ever Increasing Faith*. New Kensington, PA: Whitaker House, 2001.

Wright, Linda Raney. *Hope for the Sick and Hurting*. Nashville, TN: Thomas Nelson, 1990.